STRANGE BEDFELLOWS

OTHER BOOKS
BY HOWARD RICHLER

The Dead Sea Scroll Palindromes (1995)

*Take My Words: A Wordaholic's Guide
to the English Language* (1996)

*A Bawdy Language: How a Second-Rate Language
Slept Its Way to the Top* (1999)

Global Mother Tongue: The Eight Flavours of English (2006)

Can I Have a Word with You? (2007)

Strange Bedfellows

The Private Lives of Words

Howard Richler

RONSDALE PRESS

RONSDALE PRESS
3350 West 21st Avenue
Vancouver, BC, Canada
V6S 1G7

Typesetting: Julie Cochrane in Granjon 11.5 pt on 16
Cover Design: David Drummond
Paper: Ancient Forest Friendly "Silva" (FSC) — 100% post-consumer waste, totally chlorine-free

Ronsdale Press wishes to thank the following for their support of its publishing program: the Canada Council for the Arts, the Government of Canada through the Book Publishing Industry Development Program (BPIDP), the British Columbia Arts Council, and the Province of British Columbia through the British Columbia Book Publishing Tax Credit program.

Library and Archives Canada Cataloguing in Publication

Richler, Howard, 1948–
    Strange bedfellows : the private lives of words / Howard Richler. — 1st ed.

    ISBN 978-1-55380-100-9

    1. English language — Foreign words and phrases.
2. English language — Etymology. I. Title.

PE1582.A3R53 2010   422'.4   C2010-900570-8

At Ronsdale Press we are committed to protecting the environment. To this end we are working with Canopy (formerly Markets Initiative) and printers to phase out our use of paper produced from ancient forests. This book is one step towards that goal.

Printed in Canada by Marquis Printing, Quebec

To Leslie K. and David B.
Semper amici

ACKNOWLEDGEMENTS

I want to thank my editor Ronald Hatch
for his many useful suggestions on how to improve
the book. Many thanks as well to Carol Broderick
for her assiduous editing.

CONTENTS

INTRODUCTION

It is a good thing that words do not run for political office because many of them have histories that could cause "electile" dysfunction. Like politicians, words carry baggage, and the function of the etymologist, like the function of the muck-raking journalist, is to expose what lies disguised in the carrying cases. Alas, like people, languages occasionally sleep around, and this is why I have titled my book *Strange Bedfellows: The Private Lives of Words*. The bawdy English language, in particular, has never been overly concerned with purity, and this promiscuity has contributed to many alluring word histories. Also, like species, words evolve, and particularly those words that have been in existence for many centuries have undergone major evolutions in meaning.

When you read *Strange Bedfellows: The Private Lives of Words*, I hope you will discover the unexpected: for example, why gossiping in church is etymologically proper and why perfectly ordinary and acceptable words such as "avocado" and "porcelain" have past associations with some of the nether regions of the body that have been conveniently forgotten by the lovers of fruit and fine china.

While many word histories may not be as lurid, their origins are in any case quite surprising. Investigations show that many words have associations with other words of dubious repute, such as "gymnasium" with "nudity," and "travel" with "torture." If eggplant (aubergine in England) is not your favourite food, it may be because you have divined that it is, etymologically, an anti-fart vegetable. In the case of the association of "assassins" with "hashish-eaters," it is problematic which party should take the greater umbrage over their etymological entanglement. Also, words have roots in other languages that sometimes seem illogical, such as "alcohol" coming from Arabic, notwithstanding the Muslim prohibition of alcohol, and that all-American word "Yankee" possessing a solid Dutch pedigree.

For the most part, *Strange Bedfellows: The Private Lives of Words* is composed of chapters where I have culled ten words from specific fields whose etymologies will surprise and delight the reader. But on one special occasion I have lengthened the number from ten to two dozen, with the finale coming in at a humongous fifty-five. I could not resist.

One last comment before we turn to particular words and their liaisons, and this is to record my debt to the *Oxford English Dictionary (OED)*, which is invaluable in highlighting surprising meanings of words. The *OED* is not an ordinary dictionary but one that is based on historical principles, which is to say that it lists chronologically the different meanings of words so that the first meaning listed for a word will often diverge greatly from the dominant sense today. I wish to express my gratitude to the editors of the *OED* for their efforts in compiling what many consider the greatest work of scholarship known to mankind.

PART I
Words Stranger
than Fiction

TEN WORDS
You Never Knew Came from
Unmentionable Body Parts

People tend to name objects after things that are familiar to them, and what could be more familiar than our own bodies? The human imagination can be quite salacious, and some ingenious folks have given certain objects names that reminded them of certain body parts that, let us say, should not be mentioned when enjoying high tea in Kensington Gardens.

The eighteenth-century poet Alexander Pope wrote: "True wit is nature to advantage dressed, / what oft was thought but ne'er so well expressed." While it may be the mission of metaphor and imagination to adorn words with new meanings, it is the deconstructing duty of etymology to disrobe them.

AVOCADO

The ultimate "avocado" ancestor is *ahucatl*, "testicle," from the Aztecan language Nahuatl. The Aztecs felt that not only was the fruit shaped like a testicle, but that it possessed aphrodisiac properties. To the Spanish conquistadors, *ahucatl* proved to be a mouthful and they originally rendered it as *aguacate* and eventually moved it to *avocado*, the Spanish word at that time for "lawyer." This may explain why so many lawyers are ballsy. In any case, after the discovery of the New World, the avocado was exported to Europe where it became popular both for its taste and its supposed enhancement of the male libido. English adopted the word in 1697 and in the eighteenth century many people started calling this fruit an "alligator pear," a name still used often in the southern United States. While Nahuatl has not bequeathed many words to English, many of them are rather tasty morsels, such as "chocolate" (which has an entry all to itself in the final section), "guacamole," "chili," "tomato," "tamale," "cacao" and "chipotle."

VANILLA

In recent years, "vanilla" has acquired an adjectival sense and is used to describe something bland and perhaps uninspiring, e.g., "vanilla sex." For example, *Wikipedia* has an entry for "vanilla sex" and it asserts that "'vanilla sex' is used to describe what a culture regards as standard or conventional sexual behavior."

All I can say is, "Vanilla, we hardly knew ya." Particularly, if you are like me and vanilla represents your favourite ice cream, you may be discombobulated to discover that vanilla, etymologically, is a little vagina. Some randy Elizabethans believed that vanilla had aphrodisiac properties because of the supposed resemblance of the pod of the plant to the vagina. "Vanilla" is an extract from the Spanish *vainilla*, which means flower or pod. *Vainilla*, in turn, comes from the Spanish word *vaina*, which means sheath. *Vaina* derives from the Latin *vagina*, which means sheath for a sword. It was used lewdly as a term for the female reproductive passage.

While on the subject of words starting with the letter "V," I would be remiss if I didn't provide the vivid and alliterative description of "vulva," the external genital organ, from the *American Heritage Dictionary* — as the "vestibule of the vagina." Va-va-voom.

PORCELAIN

Alas, the bizarre history of this word leads us back to a pig's vagina. It was applied in Italian to fine china with the word *porcellana*, "cowrie shell." *Porcellana* was a derivative of *porcella*, "little sow," a form of *porca*, "sow" (to which English "pork," "porpoise" and "porcupine" are related), and was applied to cowrie shells because to some observers they resembled the wrinkled external genitalia of female pigs. In case you are wondering, "cowrie" has no connection to the word "cow" as "cowrie" derives from the Hindi and Urdu *kauri*.

TESTIFY

This word was borrowed from the Latin *testis*, "testicles." According to lore, in ancient times, a man would testify by placing his hand not on his heart, but further south on his cherished and trusted testicles. 'Twas said that should he lie, he would become impotent. I have not, however, seen compelling empirical evidence supporting this hypothesis. Because the word "testimony" is also linked to "testicle," *Ms. Magazine* received this suggestion some years ago by an outraged feminist: "I protest the use of the word 'testimony' when referring to a woman's statements, because its root is 'testes,' which has nothing to do with being a female. Why not use 'ovarimony'?" According to Francine Wattman Frank and Paula A. Treichler in *Language, Gender and Professional Writing*, this neologism is a protest against "the Islamic practice of regarding women's statements under oath as less valuable than men's."

Take that, you Taliban supporters.

PENICILLIN

This medical miracle is a derivative of the Latin word for "tail" or "paint-brush," *penicillus*, and is an allusion to the bushy nature of its spores. In

Latin, *penis* originally meant "tail" or "brush," and only by extension (pun intended) did it came to mean "male sex organ." Hence, etymologically speaking, a pencil is a little penis — you might think twice before putting that dirty chewed-on one behind your ear. The word "penis" is a latent bloomer in the English language, making its first entry in the *OED* in 1578 in anatomist John Banister's *The Historie of Man*: "They haue left a voyde, and empty corner, for the subsistyng of *Penis*, and the *Testicles*." The earliest word for the male organ I could find is "pintle," for which there is a citation in the *OED* going back to Old English.

EXUBERANT

The first definition of "exuberant" in the *OED* is "luxuriantly fertile or prolific; abundantly productive." The word blends the Latin *ex-*, "out," and *uber*, "udders," and produces *exuberans*, "overflowing udders." Notwithstanding this etymology, males are as likely as females to be characterized as exuberant, and I suspect few sows, mares or ewes are truly exuberant. In any case, knowing this etymology might make you pause before characterizing your great-aunt as an "exuberant woman."

HYSTERICAL

The Greek word for "womb" was *hystera*, and *hysterikos* meant "suffering in the womb." Our ancient forbears believed that many abnormal states of health and behaviour came about as a result of general irregularities in the body, and in particular to a nervous disorder, known as "the vapours," whose symptoms included fainting and convulsions. These ancestors (bless their patriarchal, chauvinistic hearts) felt women were more prone to this malaise as a result of a malfunction in their wombs. Even as late as 1861, we find this entry for "hysterics" in Isabella Beeton's *Book of Household Management*: "These fits take place . . . in young, nervous, unmarried women. Young women, who are subject to these fits, are apt to think that they are suffering from 'all the ills that flesh is heir to'; and the false symptoms of disease which they show are so like the true ones, that it is exceedingly difficult to detect the difference." Hence, etymologically, although not in fact, male hysteria is oxymoronic.

ORCHID

The name of this lovely flower grew out of the Greek word for "testicles," *orchis*, because of the supposed resemblance of its double root to two hairy testicles. Because of this likeness, orchids were once called "ballock stones," "ballock" (or "bollock") being a term for "testicle." An orchiectomy is not performed by a florist but rather by a urologist, and is a rather euphemistic term for castration. This might give you pause the next time you prune your orchids.

OLD HAT

Since the beginning of the twentieth century this term has referred to something that is considered old-fashioned, out of-date or unoriginal. Its original meaning, however, referred to a woman's vulva and to sexual intercourse, or to the said woman who served as the conduit of sexual gratification. The first *OED* citation in 1697 is from Thomas Durfey's *Intrigues at Versailles*: "Why, how now, ye piece of old Hat, what are ye musty? the Jade's as musty as a stale pot of Marmalade of her own making." In Francis Grose's *A Classical Dictionary of the Vulgar Tongue* published in 1796, he waggishly writes that "old hat" refers to "a woman's privities: because frequently felt." Its first usage as "old-fashioned" or "out of date" is found in Cornish writer Arthur Quiller Couch's book *Brother Copas*, written in 1911: "Men have . . . put it, with like doctrines, silently aside in disgust. So it has happened with Satan and his fork: they have become 'old hat.'"

BURK

Although "burk" is now the most common spelling, the original form was "berk." It is a shortening of "Berkeley" and derives from the

Berkeley fox hunt in Gloucestershire. The word "burk" is a British slang term for "fool," and it derives from Cockney rhyming slang. In this arcane argot, "Berkeley hunt" becomes a code for a certain age-old four-lettered word for the female pudendum, and "burk" becomes the shorthand designation in the same manner that "raspberry" designates "fart" as it represents "raspberry tart." After Rowan Williams, the Archbishop of Canterbury, in a speech in 2008 endorsed aspects of sharia law in Britain, the tabloid the *Sun* ran as its headline: "What a Burka!"

TEN WORDS
You Never Knew Came from
Mentionable Body Parts

The names of everyday objects that we take for granted were created by individuals who sometimes have been metaphorically influenced by aspects of their physiognomy and features further south. Ralph Waldo Emerson said, "Every word was once a poem." In this section we examine some of the one-word metaphors that drew inspiration from parts of our bodies.

DAISY

One would not think that the words "daisy" and "window" are paired in any manner, but an examination of their roots uncovers an ocular association. Literally, "daisy" means "day's eye." This metaphor derives from either the resemblance of a daisy to the sun or to the fact that several daisy species open in daylight hours to reveal their yellow disk, and then close once again at dusk. A window is etymologically a "wind-eye" in that it is the opening for admitting air. The word was borrowed from the Old Norse *vindauga*, a compound noun that blends *vindr*, "wind," with *auga*, "eye."

COCONUT

In a classic example of European linguistic imperialism, this tropical delight is saddled with a European name. The base of the coconut's shell, with its three small holes, apparently reminded fifteenth-century Portuguese explorers, perhaps suffering from sun stroke or scurvy, of a grinning face, as *coco* was the Portuguese word for "a smiling face."

SNITCH

While its origin is obscure, the *OED* shows that the term "snitch" referred to "nose" around the beginning of the eighteenth century. It is only in 1785 when a citation with the modern sense of "informer" appears. The English language seems to like words starting with "sn-" to be nose-related. Observe "sneeze," "sniff," "snort," "snout," "snuff," and the crypto "sn-" word "schnozz." I suppose the shift to the "informer" sense comes from the belief that one shouldn't put one's nose where it doesn't belong.

ATROCIOUS

If your performance is atrocious, it could give you a black eye — metaphorically speaking. Etymologically, however, the eye would be black, *per se*. The word "atrocious" blends Latin *ater*, "black" or "dark," and *oc*, the stem that forms the Latin word for "eye," *oculus*. Seen in this light, "ferocious" means "wild eye," as the first part of the word comes from the Latin *ferus*, "wild." While the word "atrocious" colloquially is used in the sense of "shockingly bad," its original sense in the seventeenth century was much stronger, as attested by the first *OED* definition: "Characterized by savage enormity; excessively and wantonly cruel; heinously wicked."

CORSAGE

Etymologically, the word "corsage" relates to the condition of the body, for it combines the Latin word *cors*, "body," with the noun-forming suffix *-age*. Its first two senses, appearing around the beginning of the fourteenth century, are "Bodily condition as to size and shapeliness," and "The body as distinct from the limbs; the bust." It came to refer to a bouquet worn on a bodice only towards the end of the nineteenth century.

RACQUET

"Racquet" was borrowed from the French *raquette*, "palm of the hand." In its earliest incarnation, tennis was played like handball, and the ball would be struck with the palm of the hand. In French the game was even known as *jeu de paume*, "palm game." Also, in Arabic, *rakah* means "palm of the hand."

TUTU

This word should really be placed in its own distinct category labelled "semi-mentionable body parts," as it derives from the French *cucu*, a derivative of *cul* or *cule*, "buttocks." It makes its appearance in English in 1910 in E.F. Spence's *Our Stage & Its Critics*, where it alludes to both meanings of the word: "She wished to exhibit what in technical slang is called *le tutu*, a term descriptive of the abbreviated costume and possessed also of a secondary meaning."

INOCULATE

This word is ultimately a member of the "eye" family, as the word joins the prefix *in-*, "into," with *ocul* (short for *oculus*), the Latin word for "eye." Its first citation in the *OED* is a horticultural one that goes back to the fifteenth century: "To insert (an 'eye', bud, or scion) in a plant for propagation; to subject (a plant) to the operation of budding; to propagate by inoculation." Its medical sense developed in the eighteenth century, when researchers discovered that injecting a small amount of a germ or virus into an individual could confer immunity to a disease. Although inoculation can render a germ innocuous, there is no connection between these two words aside from rendering "inoculation" as one of the most commonly misspelled words in English.

GARGOYLE

John Ayto, in *Dictionary of Word Origins*, relates that the "ancient root *gorg* originated as an imitation of throat sounds." The word "gargoyle" came into English from the Old French *gargouille*, which meant "throat" or "waterspout." It seems that the word *gargouille* came from the notion of rainwater coming out of the throats of the grotesque spouting creatures.

SARCASM

If you feel that someone is giving you lip with sarcastic comments, you are etymologically correct. The word derives from the Greek *sarkaezein*, which the *OED* describes as "to tear flesh, gnash the teeth, speak bitterly." I would think that in this process the apoplectic deliverer of vitriol just might chew his lips in a fit of rage. So you can take solace that the cutting remarks directed toward you resulted in the cut lips of its originator. In ancient Greek *sarx* meant "flesh," and we see the connection in the sister words of "sarcasm": "sarcoma," which etymologically means "to become fleshy," and "sarcophagus," which literally means "flesh-eating."

TEN WORDS
You Never Knew Were Fart-
or Fecal-Related

The *OED* notes that the word "fart" is "not in decent use." That being said, it is a word that is first recorded in (the far more than decent) Chaucer's "Miller's Tale," found in *The Canterbury Tales*: "This Nicholas anon let flee a fart." Not surprising for a word that has been embedded in our language for a long time, it has given rise to many other words such as "feisty," "fizzle," "petard" and "partridge." That the lowly fart should give rise to a large number of words should be no surprise when one recalls that excremental odours played a much larger role in earlier days when there were no bathroom deodorant sprays and electric fans to mask the smells.

FEISTY

My *Canadian Oxford Paperback Thesaurus* offers these synonyms for "feisty": "spirited, spunky, plucky, gritty, ballsy." The family history of the word, however, is not as glowing. The Old English word *fist*, meaning "to break wind," or "a foul odour," gave us our word "feisty" to describe a spirited, quarrelsome person. The spelling of this word has varied and its first citation in the *OED* occurs in 1511: "It is fartes and fyestes." "A fisting hound" was used in England as a contemptuous term for "a small dog" and "feist" is a word still used in the southern and midland dialect areas of the USA to describe a mongrel dog.

✑ FIZZLE

Also deriving from the Old English *fist* is the word "fizzle," whose original sense in the sixteenth century was "to fart without noise," what as adolescents we designated as "SBD": "silent but deadly." We read in Benjamin Walsh's 1837 translation of Aristophanes' *Knights*: "And then in court they poisoned one another with their fizzles." You may never again complain that your partner has lost his or her fizzle.

✑ PETARD

"Let it work; for 'tis the sport to have the enginer hoist with his own petard." *Hamlet*, Act 3, scene 4.

What Prince Hamlet had in mind with his usage of "petard" was an explosive device that had a tendency to explode prematurely on its deviser. The blowing up originally was probably more odoriferous but less lethal. The word "petard" derives from the French *péter* and the Latin *pedere*, both of which mean "to fart." To "peter out" means to decrease or run out of something. That this sense evolved is surprising as the word also comes from the French *péter*. The French have an expression, *Il veut péter plus haut que son cul*, which means, "He tries to appear better than he is." Literally, however, it means, "He wants to fart higher than his ass." The French have long taken a puerile pleasure in comparing this word to the English name Peter. In 1955, when Princess Margaret decided not to wed the divorced Captain Peter Townsend, a headline in a French newspaper read: "Margaret renonce à Peter" (Margaret gives up farting).

AUBERGINE

The aubergine has enjoyed an exotic etymological odyssey as an anti-fart vegetable. The Sanskrit *vatinganah* refers to the lack of gas it produces. The Sanskrit *vatinganah* bequeathed the Persian *badingan*, then the Arabic *al-badinjan*, then the Portuguese *beringela*, then the Catalan *alberginia*, which became French *aubergine*, which has been adopted by English, although in North America the designation "eggplant" is more common. In India, this vegetable is most commonly referred to as *brinjal*, and in the Caribbean this term has mutated into the merrier-sounding "brown jolly."

PARTRIDGE

At some point throughout the aeons, I'm willing to bet that a flock of partridges parted some ridges. Notwithstanding this likelihood, this said event is of no lexical significance. In ancient Greece, the slang term *perdix* (the Greek verb *perdesthai* meant "to fart") was used to describe those with a penchant for breaking wind. Apparently, the whirring of a partridge's wings reminded Greek hunters of the sound of a fart. Perhaps the "partridge in a pear tree" has an odoriferous reference?

PUMPERNICKEL

There is a folk etymology that claims that Napoleon proclaimed that pumpernickel bread was only fit for his horse, Nicol, and that this is rendered in French as *bon pour Nicol*. While we can safely discount this version, the real one is not any more appetizing. This coarse bread is the progeny of the unholy union of the New High German *pumpern*, "to break wind," and *nickel*, "goblin" or "devil." In German, "pumpernickel" once had the sense of "lout." In any event, it was claimed that if you ate pumpernickel you'd fart like the devil. According to Anatoly Liberman in *Word Origins*, words that start with "pump" or "pumper" suggest "swelling, and by implication, a full stomach. *Pumpernickel* probably got its name on account of the flatulence it causes."

POPPYCOCK

The Americanism "poppycock" is first recorded in 1865 with the sense of "humbug" in C.F. Browne's *Artemus Ward: His Travels*: "You won't be able to find such another pack of poppycock gabblers as the present Congress of the United States." Its etymology does not ameliorate the word in any sense as it derives from the Dutch *pappekak*, which means "doll's excrement." In the 1980s, the speaker of the British House of Commons ruled that its use by an honourable member was "unparliamentary." The *kak* part comes from the Latin *cacare*, "to defecate." Greek also looks askance at *kak* words because, whereas the Greek-based word "aristocracy" literally means "government by the best citizens," its antithesis, "kakistocracy," refers to a government by the worst members of society. While "poppycock" may be a gentle rejoinder, etymologically it conveys the stronger message that one's opponent is talking shit.

MISTLETOE

I hate to take the romance out of the Christmas holidays, but be forewarned that to kiss under the mistletoe might mean a smooch under a bird-shit plant. The word is cognate with the Old High German *mist*, "dung." One theory states that in days of yore people believed that mistletoe shoots came from bird droppings. Another theory postulates that the *mistil* part of "mistletoe" derives from bird-lime and not bird-dung. I suggest that squeamish Christmas canoodlers opt for the latter version.

SHYSTER

Countless etymologies have been offered for this term for a disreputable lawyer, including an unethical advocate surnamed Scheuster who lived in New York City in the 1840s. However, no such unsavoury lawyer bearing this name was registered in New York State during that era. Also, some of the purported languages of origin for this word include Dutch, German, Romany, Scottish Gaelic and Yiddish. According to

Webster's Dictionary of Word Origins the word is probably an "alteration of earlier *shicer* (contemptible fellow) from German, *scheisser*, literally, defecator." The word is first recorded in 1844, and in 1849 G. G. Foster in *New York in Slices* writes: "He must . . . wait next day for the visits of the 'shyster' lawyers — a set of turkey-buzzards whose touch is pollution and whose breath is pestilence."

✑ COWSLIP

One can divide this flower into the parts "cow's" and "lip." To do so, however, would be to slip up. The word should be divided "cow" and "slip," as the Old English *slyppe* meant "dung." The flower gets its name from its tendency to thrive in well-manured pastures.

TEN WORDS
You Never Knew Were
Originally Insults

Language and values are in a constant state of flux, and meanings of words are ever changing. Alas, even many of the seven deadly sins are no longer seen as particularly pernicious, and this has also had an effect on the meaning of words. For example, pride is now seen by virtually all to be a positive quality. Thus to express disparagement about some aspect of pride, one must use the word "hubris."

As such, we find words whose senses have almost reversed. Some words that were once not necessarily complimentary have ameliorated over the years to denote positive personality characteristics. For example, "noble" once merely referred to an accident of birth and did not imply high-mindedness.

The opposite is also true, and in this section I will look at words that we now regard as complimentary (or at least carry a somewhat positive connotation) that originally bore an insulting meaning. You will discover why, etymologically speaking, it might not matter to Santa whether you're naughty or nice.

NICE

I remember this sophomoric joke from the 1960s: What's the difference between a good girl and a nice girl? Answer: The good girl goes to a party, goes home then goes to bed whereas the nice girl goes to the party, goes to bed then goes home. Etymologically, this depiction of the nice lass is correct because the word "nice" carried a connotation of wantonness and lasciviousness many centuries before acquiring a sense of something pleasant. The word derives from the Latin *nescius*, "ignorant"; the first sense of the word at the beginning of the twelfth century was ignorant or foolish. By the end of the twelfth century this foolish behaviour could be deemed to be morally inappropriate and it acquired the sense of lasciviousness. Starting with the fourteenth century the word acquired many other senses including "extravagant," "scrupulous," "coy," "dainty" and "refined." Shakespeare in *As You Like It* (c. 1600) has Jaques speak of the lady's melancholy as being "nice," meaning fastidious. It isn't until the beginning of the eighteenth century that we see a full semantic inversion, when the word started to be used as a synonym for "respectable." By the end of the eighteenth century, Jane Austen in *Northanger Abbey* has Henry Tilney making fun of Catherine Morland for her overuse of the word: "'Very true,' said Henry, 'and this is a very nice day, and we are taking a very nice walk, and you are two very nice young ladies. Oh! It is a very nice word indeed! — It does for everything. Originally perhaps it was applied only to express neatness, propriety, delicacy, or refinement; — people were nice in their dress, in their sentiments, or their choice. But now every commendation on every subject is comprised in that one word.'" I am afraid that Henry's teasing did not do much to change the overuse of "nice." "Nice" is still the preferred adjective for anything lovely or beautiful or fine or . . . .

NAUGHTY

While being called "naughty" for the morally upright is not complimentary, its sense has definitely become less pernicious. It has come to mean "badly behaved" and it might be used to describe a child who has disregarded his or her parents' wishes. Or an actress who has done something titillating. Although its original sense in the early thirteenth century was of being needy i.e., "having naught," within fifty years the sense of being bad was not like the present one — innocuous — and it referred to a wicked or vicious person. This is the manner in which it is employed in the King James Bible, in Proverbs 6:12: "A naughty person. A wicked man, walketh with a froward mouth." This same sense is used in Shakespeare's *Henry VIII* when the King, speaking to Cranmer, the Archbishop of Canterbury, says of Jesus: "whiles here He lived / Upon this naughty earth." By the beginning of the fifteenth century, the word had acquired more than a soupçon of licentiousness and the story is told that when Samuel Johnson published his famous dictionary in 1755 he was complimented by two biddies for omitting "naughty words" in his tome. Naughty Johnson replied, "What! My dears! Then you have been looking for them!"

TORY

The term "Tory" is really an anglicized spelling of the Irish *tóraidhe*, "pursuer," and originally denoted an Irish guerilla who, to revenge being ousted from his land by the British, took to plundering Ireland's occupiers. The *OED* highlights this origin in its first definition of "Tory": "In the seventeenth century, one of the dispossessed Irish, who became outlaws, subsisting by plundering and killing the English settlers and soldiers." It quickly became a term to refer to any Irish Papist, and by the middle of the seventeenth century the word was often used by British commentators as a synonym for "bandit," as in this mid-seventeenth century reference by Bulstrode Whitelock: "Eight Officers . . . riding upon the Highway [in Ireland], were murder'd by those bloody Highway Rogues called the Tories."

At the end of the seventeenth century the word was applied to a group of English politicians who had originally opposed the deposing of

Roman Catholic King James and his replacement with the Protestant duo, William and Mary. Eventually, this loose assortment of politicians became regarded as a political party, the Tories. Even later, however, we find the word used as a derogation of the Irish. Catharine Macaulay, in *The History of England*, written in 1849 writes, "The bogs of Ireland . . . afforded a refuge to Popish outlaws, much resembling those who were afterwards known as Whiteboys. These men were then called Tories."

✐ PRETTY

In Old English, *prættig* (the forbear of "pretty") possessed a negative sense, and was synonymous with "cunning" or "crafty." It was a derivative of the word *prætt*, "trick" or "wile," and it was only in the fifteenth century that "pretty" acquired the sense of "pleasing in appearance." Even in the eighteenth century it was often used in a negative sense, as in John Arbuthnot's *John Bull*: "There goes the prettiest Fellow in the World . . . for managing a Jury." Today, when one refers to a novel as "a pretty little book," the word "pretty" can take on two meanings, depending on the emphasis given: that the book is pleasing, or very small.

✐ ELEGANT

Originally, "elegant" carried a taint of being dainty or foppish. The *OED* notes that "in early Latin *elegans* was a term of reproach, 'dainty, fastidious, foppish,' but in classical times it expressed the notions of refined luxury, graceful propriety, which are reproduced in the modern English use." The negative sense of the word can be seen in Alexander Barclay's *Ship of Fooles*, written in 1509: "It is . . . not for man to be so elegant, To such toyes wanton women may encline." Today, it is almost always positive, except in those circumstances where anything elegant is regarded as elitist.

SHREWD

The *Encarta World English Dictionary* defines "shrewd" as "good at judging people and situations." Compare this to the first definition in the *OED*: "Depraved, wicked; evil-disposed, malignant. Passing into a weaker sense: Malicious, mischievous." In *Richard II*, Shakespeare uses the word to mean "dangerous" or "harmful" when King Richard tells Aumerle, "For every man that Bolingbroke hath pressed / To lift shrewd steel against our golden crown." It is generally believed that the word comes from the mouse-like animal "shrew." During the Middle Ages many people feared this small insect-eating animal; they believed that it possessed a lethal poisonous bite and rendered cattle lame by scampering on their backs. The sense of "shrew" referring to a scolding woman comes from the image of a woman with an acid tongue and barking voice.

LUXURIOUS

Alas, there has been a shift in values, and several of the seven deadly sins such as pride and lust are not held in the same contempt as they once were, when most people were God-fearing and hell-believing souls. We see this shift in the word "luxurious." "Luxury" was originally seen as a negative quality as it denoted sinful self-indulgence. Hence the first senses of "luxurious," in 1330, according to the *OED*, are "lascivious, lecherous, unchaste." The lascivious taint of "luxury" is seen in *Hamlet* when the Prince's ghost-father tells him that the "royal bed of Denmark" is being used as "a couch for luxury and damned incest." Even as late as 1630 it carried this same sense in R. Johnson's *Kingdom and Commonwealth*: "They are exceeding luxurious, by reason whereof the Countery swarmeth with Whores."

Already by 1374, however, it had acquired another slightly less pernicious sense and could mean "outrageous, outlandish, excessive." By the seventeenth century, it had acquired a sense of habitual use of what is choice or costly, and it wasn't until the nineteenth century that it obtained its modern sense of contributing to sumptuous living.

Now that the conspicuous consumption of unregulated capitalism is endangering our resource-depleted planet, perhaps one day "luxury" will regain its rapacious sense.

PURCHASE

While in English we have the expression "buyer beware," in days of yore it was actually the purchaser who needed to be on guard. "Purchase" originally meant "to take by force." In Old French, *filz de porchaz* was a term for a bastard, and Geoffrey Hughes in *Words in Time* informs us that "For centuries *purchase* meant something far more rapacious and disorderly than the present transactional sense denotes. The old senses of *purchase*, dating in Middle English from circa 1297, were derived from *chase* and revolved around the actions of hunting and taking by force, whether the object was prey, person, plunder or pelf (stolen goods)."

FOND

Originally "fond" meant "infatuated, foolish, silly," and is used often in this sense in Shakespeare's plays. When Hamlet resolves to avenge his father's murder, he vows, "Yea from the table of my memory / I'll wipe away all trivial fond records." The same sense applies in *Julius Caesar* when Caesar tells Metellus, "Be not fond, / To think that Caesar bears such rebel blood." In *King Lear*, Lear calls himself "fond" with the sense being "foolishly affectionate." In the middle of the seventeenth century, it began to be used to mean "cherished," even by the non-foolish strains of society. Today, the word seems to be dropping a notch or two, in that it is often used as a way of not saying "love." The verb "fondle" derives from "fond," and its first usage is found at the end of the seventeenth century.

METICULOUS

Most people today would feel complimented to be called "meticulous," as it refers to someone who is extremely careful and precise, but I suppose some anarchic souls would regard it as being a tad anal-retentive. In the early nineteenth century it carried this taint of being over-careful or over-zealous, but this sense was lost towards the end of the century. When the word first appeared in the sixteenth century, however, there was no question that it carried negative associations, for it meant "fearful" or "timid," and derived from the Latin *metus*, "fear."

TWO DOZEN WORDS
You Never Knew Came
from Animals

Although I began this book with the intention that each section would be composed of ten words, I soon found that this section on animals and words could not be limited to only ten entries. Over the centuries, animals have played an extraordinary role in our lives, and thus they have enjoyed a similarly large role in word formation. There was a time when people's interactions with animals transcended the animals' appearances on plates as McNuggets or Angus Burgers. For most of our civilized history people lived in agricultural societies where one was likely to rub noses with a sheep or a pig, and animals played significant roles in one's ability to survive and flourish. People shared the same farm and often the same house with animals; one would not be surprised if at times the animals served as strange bedfellows. The ubiquity of animals is borne out by the countless expressions that relate to animals, such as a "bird in the hand," "counting chickens," "bull in a china shop," "white elephant," "sleeping dogs," and so on. Also when faced with giving a name to a new word in English that provided a particular function, people found it natural to name that word after an animal that dispensed a somewhat similar function. This is what happened in the cases of the words "easel" and "bidet" (if you don't recognize the animal, then read on). Since one co-existed with animals, it was natural that when a new word was needed it was named after some seemingly ever-present critter.

———✿———

I'm beginning the "Animals" section with livestock to recognize the importance they have played in our existence as essential aids in the agricultural process. For most of our recorded history, agriculture was the key development that led to the rise of human civilization, with the husbandry of domesticated animals and plants creating food surpluses that enabled the development of more densely populated areas. Between the eighth century and the eighteenth, the tools of farming basically stayed the same and few advancements in technology were made. A revolution in agricultural development occurred between the start of the eighteenth century and the end of the nineteenth century, and this period saw a massive and rapid increase in agricultural productivity and vast improvements in farm technology. In this section you will discover why it is indeed not peculiar that the word "peculiar" is related to livestock.

✐ SCREW

The noun "screw" (our familiar fastener with the sharp point and spiral ridges) comes from the Old French *escroue*, which bequeathed the modern French *écrou*, or "nut." However, the word ultimately comes from the Latin *scrufa*, "sow." Katherine Barber in *Six Words You Never Knew Had Something to Do with Pigs* speculates that it was the curly tail that people had in mind when they made the connection between a female pig and a screw. Both have the same spiral shape. I have been informed, however, by an acquaintance who owns a pig farm that what is screwy about a boar is not his tail but his penis, which comes equipped with a screw tip that he literally screws into the cervix of the sow.

BUGLE

The first definition of "bugle" in the *OED* goes back to the fourteenth century, and means "the buffalo and other kinds of wild oxen." This seems odd until we remember that the Latin word for ox is *bos* and one of its diminutives is *buculus*. In Old French *buculus* became transmogrified as *bugle*, the archaic word for "buffalo." But how did a buffalo come to refer to a musical instrument? The answer is found in the second definition of "bugle" that emerged forty years after the first: "A hunting-horn, originally made of the horn of a 'bugle' or wild ox."

BULIMIC

Although the late Princess Diana was given to bouts of bulimia, not many would associate her with an ox. Her graceful mien would seem to be anything but ox-like. It pains us to relate, however, that bulimia is a blend of our aforementioned Greek *bos*, "ox," and *limos*, "hunger." Given that bulimia is associated with excessive eating (etymologically a bulimic eats like an ox), which is a hallmark of our modern body-conscious age, it is surprising to find what a long lineage the word possesses. Already in 1398, English writer John de Trevisa was writing: "Bolismus is inmoderate and inmesurable as it were an houndes appetyte."

PECULIAR

If you find it peculiar that a musical instrument such as a bugle derives from a type of ox, it is equally peculiar that the word "peculiar" itself has a connection to cows. In Latin the word *pecu* means "cattle" and since cattle are property (in ancient Rome before the minting of coins, "pecuniary" cattle took the place of money), the word *peculiaris* means "privately owned." The sense of "peculiar" — meaning "something strange" — developed from the concept that one's property was distinctive. Daniel Defoe used "peculiar" in this sense in 1724 in *Tour Through the Whole Island of Great Britain*: "This Square . . . is separated, and Peculiar to the Wholesale Dealers in the Woollen Manufacture." Today's dominant sense of the word — as "singular," "unusual," "strange," or "odd" — emerged a century before Defoe, and the first example has nothing to do with cows, but serpents. In his *History of Serpents*, Edward Topsell in 1608 comments that "the Tongue of a Serpent is peculiar, for . . . it is also clouen at the tippe." Not the sinister, cunning serpent, but the peculiar serpent.

﹏ TRAGEDY

In ancient Greece the word for "goat" was *tragos*, and the word for singer, *oide*. These elements blended to form *tragoidia*, "tragedy." We see the song-like *oide* element today in words such as "rhapsody," "parody" and "ode." Nobody knows for sure why a tragedy is etymologically a goat song, but theories abound. Perhaps goats were given as prizes at ancient Greek dramatic festivals, or actors at these festivals dressed in goatskins. Or perhaps the origin lies in goats being sacrificed at dramatic religious rituals — a true tragedy if you happened to be a goat.

﹏ CAPRICE

Nineteenth-century British writer Thomas De Quincy opined, "Everywhere I observe in the feminine mind something of a beautiful caprice, a floral exuberance of that charming willfulness which characterizes our dear human sisters." Needless to say De Quincy was not being complimentary in referring to what he saw as the essential impulsive tendencies of women. Women, however, would probably be more offended to know that etymologically their caprice makes them goat-like. The word derives from the Italian *capriccio*, which itself comes from the Latin *caper*, "goat." Shakespeare puns on the bovine origin of the word in *As You Like It* when he has Touchstone woo Audrey with the words: "I am heere with thee, and thy Goats, as the most capricious Poet, honest Ovid, was among the Gothes." The sentence contains a triple pun since in Shakespeare's time the word "goats" was pronounced very much like "Gothes" and, as has been seen, the word "capricious" also contains the meaning of "goat."

VACCINE

"Vaccine" was adapted from the Latin *vaccinus*, which means literally "of a cow." It was used by British physician Edward Jenner at the end of the eighteenth century in the term "vaccine disease" for "cowpox." The history of the smallpox vaccine is especially interesting and very much tied to cows. When Jenner noticed that milkmaids did not generally contract smallpox, he suggested that the pus in the blisters that the milkmaids developed from the disease cowpox (which was a much less virulent than smallpox) protected them from smallpox. He then began successfully inoculating people with the cowpox from the blisters of milkmaids. The word "vaccine" itself was not used as a noun meaning "matter used in inoculation" until 1846.

JUBILEE

Perhaps a jubilee is a time to be jubilant, but the word bears no etymological ode to joy. The first definition of this word in the *OED* is "A year of emancipation and restoration, which according to the institution in Leviticus XXV was to be kept every fifty years, and to be proclaimed by the blast of trumpets throughout the land; during it the fields were to be left uncultivated, Hebrew slaves were to be set free, and lands and houses in the open country or unwalled towns that had been sold were to revert to their former owners or their heirs."

This august year takes its name from the Hebrew word *yobhel*, "ram's horn," which was used to proclaim the advent of this event. The word "jubilee" is first used in John Wycliffe's 1382 translation of the Bible: "Thow shalt halowe the fyftith yeer . . . he is forsothe the iubilee." Chaucer was the first person to use the word without its religious context and by the late sixteenth century its secular sense became the dominant meaning.

✐ STEWARD

"Steward" can refer to someone who manages property or a shop or to someone who attends to passengers' needs on a plane or a ship. Its first sense in the *OED* goes back to the year 1000 and is defined as "an official who controls the domestic affairs of a household, supervising the service of his master's table, directing the domestics, and regulating household expenditure." The first element of the word, the *ste-* part, tells us that what is being "warded" over is a "sty." In those days a man's wealth was registered by the size of his pigsty. Etymologically, it is small wonder that female flight attendants don't want to be referred to as stewardesses. Alas, my own first name, "Howard," may have arisen as a shortening of "hog's warden."

Turning now to horses, we know that the domestication of horses took place somewhere between 4500 BC and 2000 BC and probably first occurred in central Asia. We should not forget that before the advent of the automobile, horsepower was provided solely by horses and donkeys.

✐ CURTAIL

True or false: "Curtail" comes from the practice of cutting dogs' tails. If you answered "false," you are correct, but only because the word derives from the docking of the tail of a horse, not a dog. The *OED* relates that the archaic word "curtal" refers to "A horse with its tail cut short or docked, and sometimes the ears cropped." "Curtail" was borrowed in the sixteenth century from the French *courtault*, which derives from the word for "short," *court*.

BIDET

For those unsophisticated souls who have never stayed at a Parisian hotel, I should explain that a bidet is a low bathroom plumbing fixture equipped with a spray of water that is used for washing the genitalia and the posterior. In the fourteenth century there existed an Old French verb *bider*, "to trot," that begat the noun *bidet*, a small pony or a donkey. Its first meaning in English is recorded in 1630 as "a small horse" in Ben Jonson's masque *Chloridia*: "I will return to myself, mount my bidet, in a dance, and curvet upon my curtal." It only acquired the bathroom fixture sense more than a century later. One can only assume that someone with an active imagination named the bidet after the pony because one had to pull up one's knees while cleansing the nether regions as one does when riding a small pony.

EASEL

I suppose an easel renders painting easier for an artist, but it nevertheless bears no etymological connection with "ease." The word "easel" comes from the Dutch *ezel*, "donkey." The word's creator must have likened the supportive nature of the wooden frame used to hold a picture to the load-bearing nature of the beast of burden. As was noted earlier, there is a tendency in language to name objects that provide a service after animals. Observe "sawhorse" and "monkey wrench." In French, an easel is called *un chevalet*, "wooden horse."

〰 WALLOP

Although it doesn't even rhyme with "gallop," the word "wallop" shares a common root. Both words can be traced back to the Frankish *walahlaupan*, "jump well," and came into Old French as *galoper* and then into English as "gallop." In the northern dialect of Old French it was rendered as *waloper* and naturally enough later into English as "wallop." From the fourteenth to the sixteenth centuries English equestrians would merrily "wallop" through the hills and dales. This "w" sound proved difficult for the folks back in France and hence *waloper* became *galoper* in Parisian French. The English, ever emulating trends out of Paris, then decided to "gallop" rather than "wallop" their horses. Meanwhile, "wallop" went through a series of meaning changes. It came to refer to rapid boiling, then to a noisy movement of the body, and only in 1823 did it begin to refer to a resounding blow. The British refer to alcoholic beverages as "wallops," perhaps because they can wallop you if you are not careful.

〰 BACHELOR

Nineteenth-century American punster Ambrose Bierce wisecracked that a bachelor was "A man who never had a bride idea." Yet, according to the *OED*, "bachelor" derives from the Latin *baccalaria* and is probably related to the Latin word for "cow," *bacca*, or *vacca*. Also, a *baccalarius* referred to a person employed on a grazing farm, though it is unlikely that the *baccalarius* was conferred any academic degree as a result of a passing mark in sheep grazing. In any case this ovine connection might somewhat diminish your excitement over being invited to bachelor parties. From this bucolic origin, the word took on many other associations of inexperience over the generations, such as "young knight," "junior member of a trade guild" and in 1362 it is recorded with the sense of someone who takes the lowest degree at a university. In "The Squire's Tale" of 1386, Chaucer extended the sense of inexperience to unmarried men: "Yong, fressh, strong, and in Armes desirous, / As any Bacheler of al his hous," although here the inexperience is certainly dedicated to experience.

AMNIOTIC

The "amnion" is the innermost membrane enclosing the fetus before birth. This word, as well as "amniotic," derives from the ancient Greek word for lamb, *amnos*. So why does "amniotic" derive from lamb? Because a lamb is the animal usually offered for sacrifice, and an amnion serves as a basin to collect the blood from the sacrifice.

For those of us who are not football fans, we associate lions and bears with the concept of fierceness. This is borne out in the following entry with the word "berserk" associated with blood-lust, and the word "abet," whose etymology is connected to bloodthirstiness. On the other hand, you will see how a gentle flower was inspired by the king of beasts.

BERSERK

Berserkr was a hero in Norse mythology who possessed great strength and ferocious courage. It was said that he fought on the battlefield with a frenzied fury known as the "berserker rage," emulated by Sylvester Stallone in his *Rambo* flicks. The word only found its way into the English language when the erudite Sir Walter Scott used it in a footnote to his 1822 novel *The Pirate*. Most etymologists believe that *ber serkr* derives from *bern* (bear) *serkr* (coat) or "bear's coat," as it is common in many mythologies for warriors to wear the skins of animals.

DANDELION

A dandelion was originally called a "lion's tooth" as the indented leaf of the plant was seen to resemble a lion's tooth, but in the sixteenth century the term "dandelion" caught on as it comes from *dent de lion*, the French way of saying "lion's tooth." Ironically, although English adopted the word "dandelion" from French, the French do not call a dandelion *une dent de lion* but refer, not to its shape, but to the diuretic property that people believe the flower possesses. Hence, it is called in French *pissenlit*, "wet the bed." The word "pissabed" is found in many English dictionaries as an alternative word for "dandelion."

ABET

"Abet" derives from that crowd-pleasing, blood-lusting Elizabethan diversion of bear baiting, where a starved bear was chained to a stake and a pack of dogs was set loose upon it in a fight to the death. Spectators who urged the dogs on were said to "abet" them, "abet" being the contraction of the Old French *abeter*, "to bait." Today of course it has more the meaning of to encourage or assist, interestingly enough, often to encourage an offender.

According to archaeological and genetic evidence, man's best friend, the dog, evolved from a tamed wolf around 15,000 years ago. Wolves and humans shared some traits. We were both hunters inclined to hunt in packs, and occasionally we would hunt each other, and eat each other. Hence there was a practical reason for taming wolves and transforming them into cuddly dogs who would eat our garbage rather than eating us.

TUXEDO

A tuxedo is sometimes called a penguin suit or monkey suit. If you avoid wearing one because you don't want to be linked with these unimposing animals, you will be comforted to learn that the jacket could align you etymologically with a fierce wolf. We obtained "tuxedo" from a Native

American word for wolf, *ptuksit*. In the eighteenth century, Ptuksit was also the name of a village in southeast New York State and this was anglicized first as "Tucksito" and then as "Tuxedo." Near the turn of the twentieth century, young male socialites in Tuxedo, New York, eschewing the current fashion, started to wear dress jackets, without tails. The new style that they helped popularize came to be known as a "tuxedo."

HARASS

Nowadays one can be harassed in any number of ways, and the word refers to any persistent hounding of someone. Although I suppose that people have been harassed in a sexual manner since time immemorial, the term "sexual harassment" only came into vogue in the 1970s. Originally, however, the sense of the word "harass" was restricted to hounds, for the word derives from the Old French *harer*, "to set a dog on." This verb came from the Old French *hare*, an urging to dogs during a hunt. Etymologically, it is not connected to the verb "to harry," which means "to harass."

Insects and rodents tend to be disparaged in the English language. Observe the connotations of words such as "rat," "weasel," "shrew," "insect" and "bug." While you might think of them as uninspiring critters, be aware that they have inspired us to create many words in their honour ranging from nervous and noisy people ("ukulele" and "paparazzi") to foods ("vermicelli") and body parts ("muscle").

UKULELE

In Hawaiian, the word *ukulele* blends the word *uku*, "jumping," to *lele*, "flea." While there is no resemblance between the insect and the instrument, there was a supposed similarity between the instrument's progenitor and the flea. I speak of Edward Purvis, a nineteenth-century British army officer who was attached to the court of Hawaiian King Kalakua. In 1879, some Portuguese immigrants to Hawaii brought with them the machete, a small four-stringed guitar popular in Portugal and Madeira. Purvis was enthralled by this instrument, and before long he became quite adept at playing it. Since Purvis was a diminutive, jumpy man, his nickname was *ukulele*, or "one who jumped like a flea," and because Hawaiians associated this new instrument with him, they renamed this instrument using his nickname.

MUSCLE

I, for one, while sober, never associate a muscle with a mouse, but this is how "muscle" was named. In Latin, the word for "mouse" is *mus*. Our Latin-speaking forbears, given to Bacchanalian tendencies, must have believed that the shape and movement of certain muscles, like those of the upper arm, were reminiscent of a quivering mouse. So they made up the word *musculus*, which means "little mouse," and from the word *musculus* we get "muscle." This relationship is found in some other languages. For example, in Greek, *pontiko* means both "mouse" and "muscle," and in German, *maus* also refers to both. Similarly, in Russian, Serbo-Croatian and Arabic, the words for "mouse" and "muscle" are connected.

PAPARAZZI

This word (the plural of *paparazzo*) was popularized after the tragic death of Princess Diana, whom we encountered earlier in this chapter in the entry BULIMIC. "Paparazzi" comes directly from the name of Signore Paparazzo, a photographer in Federico Fellini's 1960 film *La Dolce Vita*. In turn, the fictional character's name comes from an Italian dialect word for a noisy, buzzing mosquito. There are several versions of why Fellini named his photographer Paparazzo. Fellini claims that the surname was taken from an opera libretto, but some sources claim that the film director had known a frenetic fellow nicknamed Paparazzo during his school days and likened his photographer to this person. Still another theory postulates that the name came from Coriolano Paparazzo, a person mentioned by George Gissing in his 1901 travel book *By the Ionian Sea*. It is alleged that Fellini's script writer read the book and borrowed the name for the photographer.

VERMICELLI

Vermicelli is a kind of pasta made in the form of long, slender threads. Although quite tasty, its name might put off the etymologically squeamish, as it is related to "vermin," being the plural of the Italian *vermicello*, diminutive of *verme*, "worm." It is so named because when heated it expands and exudes what resembles small worms.

TEN WORDS
You Never Knew Came from Religion

I believe it is a fair assumption that in days gone by, religion, like animals, played a larger role in the lives of individuals. As such, it is not surprising that many words derive from religion. It was perhaps not more than a century ago, when the most common euphemisms in the English language were religious ones and God-fearing souls sounded "zounds" instead of "by God's wounds," "gadzooks" instead of "God's hooks," "doggone" instead of "goddamn" and "tarnation" instead of "damnation." Over time many originally religious-based words have lost any hint of their theological bases in our ever more secular society. For example, a "parlour" originally referred to an apartment in a monastery or a convent in which residents could talk amongst themselves or with people from outside the establishment. Here are ten deconstructed temporal words with their religious roots unearthed.

GOSSIP

The first definition of this word in the *OED* suggests what we today would term a "godfather" or "godmother": "One who has contracted spiritual affinity with another by acting as a sponsor at a baptism." The etymology of this word is more understandable once we realize that the first syllable comes from "God" and the second from "sib," as in "sibling." Queen Elizabeth I (the Elizabeth immortalized on screen by Cate Blanchett, not Helen Mirren) was the "gossip" at the baptism of James VI of Scotland. Shakespeare uses the word in this sense in *Two Gentleman of Verona*. It must have been felt that there was too much chattering at christenings because by the seventeenth century the dominant sense of the word became "newsmonger."

CRETIN

Employing this word to refer to an idiot should be banned by all upright etymologically minded Christians, for the term *creitin*, or *crestin*, was used in the Swiss Alps to refer to someone afflicted with mental weakness and stunted growth who, it was believed, would retain a child-like innocence that would protect him or her from committing grave sins. It would not take long for the "fools of God" to be regarded as merely fools. This originally kind word passed into French as *cretin* meaning "idiot" and has acquired the same narrow, pejorative sense in English.

HALIBUT

In Middle English (the English spoken after the Norman Invasion of 1066) we find the term "butte" and this survives in modern English as "butt," a word that describes many kinds of flatfish such as sole, turbot or halibut. As fish was often served on holy days, "butte" was grafted onto "haly" (a form of "holy") and this gave us the Middle English "halybutte," that became the Modern English "halibut." And you thought mackerel was holy.

PRETZEL

Jay Jacobs, in *The Eaten Word*, relates that "in Medieval monasteries, pretzels were served to young scholars, to remind them of arms crossed in prayer." There is, unfortunately, no proof that pretzels are twisted in order to emulate folded, praying arms, notwithstanding that it would make for a more savoury snack at mass than a wafer. Ultimately, the word comes from the German *bretzel*, a kind of bread roll, made from a thin length of dough twisted into a knot and coated with brine before baking. These are quite different from the small crisp pretzels that are now served on airplane flights instead of nuts. In baseball, a curve ball is sometimes referred to as a "pretzel curve." Why pretzels were originally made in the shape of a knot (and still are) we don't know.

ENTHUSIASM

The first definition of "enthusiasm" in the *OED* is "Possession by a god, supernatural inspiration, prophetic or poetic frenzy; an occasion or manifestation of these." The root of the word is the Greek word for God, *theos*; in Greek *entheos* means "possessed" or "inspired," and when the word "enthusiasm" was first used in the late sixteenth century, the religious sense was retained. Already by the seventeenth century, however, the term had come to mean "fancied inspiration." In 1660, the philosopher Henry More wrote in *Explanations of the Grand Mystery of Godliness*, "If ever Christianity be exterminated, it will be by Enthusiasm." Samuel Johnson's *Dictionary* described it as "a vain confidence of divine favour." By the nineteenth century, the dominant sense of the word had been secularized and in definition 3a, the *OED* states that "enthusiasm" in its principal current sense refers to "rapturous emotion kindled by a passionate pursuit of an interest." In a similar fashion, around one thousand years ago, the word "giddy" meant "possessed by a god" and only came to mean "dizzy" at the end of the sixteenth century.

SHRIFT

"Shrift" is one on those fossilized words such as "kith" and "fangled" whose existence is contingent on it being grafted onto another word.

Shakespeare, however, had other options for the word. In *Romeo and Juliet*, Juliet's nurse asks her young mistress, "Have you got leave to go to shrift today?" In this context, "shrift" referred to the confession of sins and the granting of absolution. To receive "short shrift" meant one wasn't getting the attention one merited. At times, "short shrift" alluded to an even more precarious situation, and this was the sense alluded to by Shakespeare's Duke in *Measure for Measure* when he says, "I will give him a present shrift, and advise him for a better place." Here "shrift" refers to the short period of time allotted to some poor sod to make his confession before being executed. The past participle of "shrift" was "shriven," and this word lives on in the associated adjective "shrove" as in Shrove Tuesday, the Tuesday before Ash Wednesday. It is often called Pancake Day, and refers to a time of merriment.

✑ BEAD

The original meaning of "bead" is "prayer" and this sense is found in English before the year 1000. Because the order and the number of beads were kept on what nowadays is called a rosary, which is a string of small balls, the word "bede" (later "bead") came to be applied to the balls themselves. In Middle English, a "beadsman" referred to someone who prayed for people's souls. One wonders if the name of the monk, the Venerable Bede, who completed the first serious work of English history in 731, derives from his profession.

✑ MAUDLIN

"Maudlin" is merely an alteration of Magdalen who, if you remember your New Testament or *The Da Vinci Code*, is the designation of a certain Mary who hailed from Magdala on the Sea of Galilee. In the Middle Ages she is usually portrayed in paintings as weeping. It was then applied in the seventeenth century to those who became drunk and fell into fits of tearful sentimentality and gross displays of affection.

It soon crept over into its more modern meaning, acquiring the sense of being sentimental in a shallow manner, often with tears flowing liberally.

PATTER

The word "glib" shows up in several dictionary entries for the headword "patter." Such heresy! This word comes from *Pater Noster*, the first Latin words in the Lord's Prayer. In the fourteenth century, Chaucer uses "patter" to mean to repeat a prayer in a rapid and mechanical fashion, and before long this indistinct, mumbling form of recitation was applied to areas other than prayer. Henry Wadsworth Longfellow's poem "Midnight Mass for the Dying Year" alludes to both senses of "patter" when he says: "The hooded clouds, like friars, / Tell their beads in drops of rain/ And patter their doleful prayers."

PRECARIOUS

If your wishes have been granted as a result of a supplication to God, etymologically, you are in a precarious situation, for *precarius* in Latin means "obtained by prayer." The Latin *precarius* comes from *prex*, "prayer" or "entreaty." The modern sense of "precarious" meaning "unsafe" derives from the reality that not all prayers are answered to the satisfaction of the supplicant.

TEN WORDS
You Never Knew Came
from the Military

Sadly the scourge of war has always been with us. As a small consolation, it has provided us with new words that have enriched our language. Many military words are quite evocative, and over time they have been generalized and have acquired non-military meanings. One such word is "rally," which originally referred to a rapid reassembling of a military force and now can refer to a gathering replete with cheerleaders designed to inspire a high-school football team.

As a side note, although the French have the reputation of preferring making love to making war, many terms that originally had a military sense such as "bivouac," "barricade" and "campaign" originated in French, as well as several not-so-obvious words of military lineage that will be explored here.

GRAPEVINE

Thanks to singer Marvin Gaye and others, we think of a "grapevine" as the metaphorical route through which a rumour passes. Interestingly, in

World War I, this information must have been passed on in outhouses as it was referred to as a "latrine rumour." Unlike its present symbolic sense, the original meaning of "grapevine" was quite literal and was a shortening of "grapevine telegraph." The first one was constructed just prior to the American Civil War by attaching wires to trees. Over time, the wire would lose its tautness and lie on the ground, presumably resembling a wild grapevine. During the war, similar lines were laid by troops and since the reports heard over these lines were unreliable, the word "grapevine" came to refer to an unsubstantiated rumour.

DEADLINE

Journalists who have problems dealing with deadlines can take comfort that the word used to refer to a far graver situation. The first definition of "deadline" in the *OED* is "a line drawn around a military prison, beyond which a prisoner is liable to be shot down." Again we have an American Civil War origin. At the Confederate camp at Andersonville, Georgia, a line was actually marked out some distance from the outer wire fence. Any prisoner crossing this line was shot on sight. This doesn't sound very civil to me.

According to American sociologist Irving Lewis Allen, the term also referred to a line on Fulton Street in Manhattan whose crossing by any known swindler in the year 1880 would result in the arrest of the said inveigler. Apparently by the end of this decade Manhattan's 14th Street was informally referred to as the "deadline."

By the 1920s, the term had mellowed somewhat and was applied to non-lethal time limits.

WARDROBE

This word that descends from Old French has shifted away from its initial military sense. In Old French it was rendered as *warderobe*, and referred to a compartment used to store and guard ("ward") valuables ("robe") captured from the enemy.

ALARM

If we are alarmed, we should spring to arms because that is what the Italian *all'arme* meant. Later the Italians rendered it as *allarme*, and over time the sense of the word shifted from a military command to the sense of panic one has on hearing this clarion call. By the sixteenth century the word was used to refer to a mechanical device — such as a watch or a clock — that sounds the alarm.

LOOPHOLE

In the thirteenth century, a "loop" referred to a narrow window and thus, originally, a "loophole" referred to the narrow vertical opening in medieval fortifications through which soldiers could fire their missiles. The invention of gunpowder diminished the military efficacy of these openings and the word came to refer to any small opening in a wall. By 1663, it is used in a metaphorical sense to refer to an outlet or means of escape. A correspondence by poet Andrew Marvell in this year relates, "It would be much below You and Me . . . to have such loop-holes in Our souls, and to . . . squeeze Our selves through our own words." In 1704, satirist Thomas Brown first used it in the sense it is often used today — a legal ambiguity which one can use to one's advantage: "Some of the Doctor's Counsel has found out a Loop-hole for him in the Act."

SLOGAN

If your favourite slogan is "Make love — not war" you are etymologically off base. The word "slogan" comes from the Gaelic *sluagh* for "army" and *ghairm* for "shout" and originally referred to a war cry of the old Highland clans that usually consisted of a personal surname or of a gathering place. It became generalized in the early eighteenth century to refer to a distinctive cry or phrase of any person or group of people. By 1859, Thomas Macaulay was using "slogan" in its modern meaning when he says in his *History of England*, "The popular slogans on both sides were indefatigably repeated."

✑ AVANT-GARDE

Particularly in the arts, the term *avant-garde* has been used since the early twentieth century to characterize innovation in particular fields. But back in 1485, in Thomas Malory's *Le Morte D'Arthur*, it possessed a military sense. The *OED*'s first definition is as the "foremost part of an army," in other words, its advance guard. Even as late as 1800, poet Samuel Taylor Coleridge uses the term in its military sense in his translation of Schiller's play *The Death of Wallenstein*.

✑ BOULEVARD

This word comes from the same source as "bulwark," the German *bollwerk*. According to Christine Ammer's *Fighting Words*, in medieval France, a *boulevard* (originally rendered as *boulevart* or *boulever*) referred to the top of a rampart that could stretch over twenty feet wide and served as the defensive walls of towns. When more sophisticated weaponry rendered this protection obsolete, the edifice was sometimes razed to ground level and used as a wide avenue. The old city of Vienna has a wide boulevard called the Ring that circles the old town on the site of the original city walls. In North America, boulevards are either wide streets, sometimes with a lawn down the middle, or the grassy swath between the sidewalk and the road.

✑ CARTE BLANCHE

This term that literally means "white paper" began as a military term referring to unconditional surrender. A defeated army leader would be forced to sign his name to a blank piece of paper on which the victor wrote whatever terms of surrender he so desired. In 1707, L. Raby in *The Hearne Collection* states, ". . . who sent Chart Blanch to make a Peace." By the late eighteenth century the concept of unconditional authority spread beyond a military use. Today it means complete freedom to act as one thinks best.

BLOCKBUSTER

"Blockbuster" originated as slang during World War II when the British Royal Air Force designated very large bombs (as much as 8,000 pounds) as "blockbusters" because of their capability to destroy entire city blocks of buildings. The September 29, 1942, issue of *Time* magazine reported: "Inside a sturdy observation tower a mile from the exploding 'block busters' which the Army is now testing at the Aberdeen Proving Ground. . . ." After the war ended, "blockbuster" became Madison Avenue-ese for a film, book or play that achieves enormous commercial success.

TEN WORDS
You Never Knew Came
from Foods

Nineteenth-century French politician, gastronome and writer Anthelme Brillat-Savarin penned, "Tell me what you eat, and I will tell you what you are." It would appear that many words owe their existence to particular foods or to the means of preparing the food. This is indeed food for thought.

LORD & LADY

Some of our oldest and most common words are among the most poetic. Take the duo of "lord" and "lady." Both these words began in Old English as *hlaf*, "bread." A lord is etymologically "the guardian of the bread," whereas the lady is the "kneader of the bread." The former was originally referred to as the *hlafweard* (the last syllable giving us "ward") and this transformed eventually into "lord." Similarly, "lady" derived from *hlafdige*, whose last syllable gave us "dough."

BUCCANEER

The Tainos of Haiti used a framework of sticks for roasting meat that the Spanish rendered as *barbacoa*. This word came to refer to the cooking of the meat itself and came into the English language as "barbecue." This technique of cooking was called *boucan* by other tribes in the Caribbean region, and this word surfaces in the *OED*'s first definition of "buccaneer": "One who dries and smokes flesh on a boucan after the manner of the Indians." Pirates often bought dried meat from these "boucaniers" and eventually the term "boucanier" or "buccaneer" was applied to the pirates.

COCKNEY

The first definition of "cockney" in the *OED* is "An egg: the egg of the common fowl, hen's egg; or perhaps one of the small or misshapen eggs occasionally laid by fowls, still popularly called in some parts 'cocks' eggs.'" Chaucer uses the word in this manner in "The Reeve's Tale." During the sixteenth century, the term was used by country folk to refer to city dwellers considered ignorant of the established customs and mainly rural ways. It was said that these city slickers couldn't tell the difference between a good egg and a cockney, a small egg with no yolk. This term in due course became synonymous with working class Londoners themselves. It also has a geographical sense in that it is applied to those living in east London. Traditionally, a cockney was one who lived within the sound of Bow bells. It has now almost lost its once denigrating connotation — but look out if you call someone with a plummy accent a cockney.

SALARY

If you are fortunate enough to still have a job and are exuding saline sweat, blood and tears to earn the salary on which income tax is based, you are etymologically correct. In Roman times, when salt was not easy to obtain and served the purpose of maintaining as well as enhancing the savour of food, it was so highly valued that soldiers were allowed a sum of money to buy it. Later this money, called *salarium*, came to refer to the stipend paid to the soldiers. Hence, if you are indeed earning your salary, you are "worth your salt." Another word that etymologically is salt-related is "salad," as the original salads in the late fifteenth century were usually seasoned with salt.

SHIBBOLETH

A "shibboleth" refers to a catchword that marks one as a member of a group. Originally, exclusion from this select group could prove deadly. "Shibboleth" in Hebrew seemingly had the innocuous meaning of an "ear of corn." It was a word that proved difficult for some to pronounce. Judges 12:5–6 tells us:

> The Gileadites took the passages of Jordan before the Ephraimites; and it was so, that when those Ephraimites which were escaped said; Let me go over; that the men of Gilead said unto him, Art thou an Ephraimite? If he said, Nay: Then said they unto him, Say now Shobboleth: and he said Sibboleth: for he could not . . . pronounce it right. Then they took him, and slew him at the passages of Jordan.

The *OED* points out that increasingly in the twentieth century, the word is used to refer to "a moral formula held tenaciously and unreflectingly, especially a prohibitive one; a taboo." Noel Coward uses it in this sense in *Private Lives*: "All the futile moralists. . . . Laugh at them. . . . Laugh at everything, all their sacred shibboleths."

COMPANION/COMPANY

Etymologically, "companion" and "company" both refer to the act of sharing bread with others as they are composed of the parts *cum*, "together," and *panis*, "bread." A "pantry," etymologically, is a room where bread is stored. In the late fourteenth century, the word "company" was applied to trade guilds and by the sixteenth century it was applied to an association formed to carry on some commercial or industrial undertaking. I suppose it can be said that those involved in this latter form of company hope there will be a lot of "bread" to share.

BUBKES

This word (sometimes rendered as "bobkes" and "bupkiss") comes from Russian where it means "beans" and, in some dialects, the less scrumptious "rabbit shit." It is used in Yiddish and Yiddish-English to mean "nothing" and is usually uttered in a scornful tone. Although the word is prevalent (particularly in New York City), and the word in its many spelling incarnations receives over 80,000 Google hits. When I began this volume it was still not found in the *OED*. But by June of 2009, I discovered that the editors had added "bupkis" to its arsenal with these alternate spellings: bobkes, bobkis, bopkes, bopkus, bubkes, bubkess, bubkis, bubkiss, bupkes, bupkis, bupkiss and bupkus. It is defined as "absolutely nothing, nil."

ALIMONY

If you are paying out alimony, it may be worth reflecting that, etymologically speaking, "alimony" means "eating money," as it derives from the Latin *alimonia*, "nutriment." It is first found in English in the seventeenth century with the sense of "maintenance." Almost immediately, it acquired the specific sense of the money a wife is entitled for sustenance from her husband after a divorce. Now that women are frequently earning more than men, it will be interesting to see if the term is enlarged to cover the provision a wife pays a husband after a divorce.

BOWEL

If sausage represents one of your favourite foods, it behooves me to relate that your bowels are etymologically "little sausages." The word comes from the Latin *botellus*, which meant "intestine" or "little sausage." It is said that the Romans used the same word for both because soldiers noticed a distinct resemblance of the slashed stomachs of their slain comrades to sausages. Moreover sausages used to be stuffed into the intestines of animals, in the same way that a sheep's stomach was used as the covering for haggis.

YANKEE

Most etymologists believe the term comes from *Jan Kees*, a version of *Jan Kaas*, "John Cheese," a derogatory designation for one of Dutch ancestry. Another theory has the word deriving from the Dutch *Janke*, a diminutive of *Jan*, "John." The first usage of the term "Yankee" was as a pejorative term for American colonials, used by the British military. In 1758, General James Wolfe used this term to express his low opinion of the American troops assigned to him. It was not until the Battle of Lexington, the first skirmish in the American Revolution in 1775, that Americans began applying the word "Yankee" to themselves and wearing the nickname with pride. A 1775 *OED* citation confirms this with the editor's note that follows the citation: "Yankies — a term formerly of derision, but now merely of distinction, given to the people of the four eastern states."

TEN WORDS
You Never Knew Came
from Mythology

In 1983, lexicographer Adrian Room wrote: "Many of the most familiar names of classical mythology have long been firmly rooted in our literary consciousness, where they usually rank on a popular par with Biblical figures and the more memorable characters in Shakespeare's plays." Room adds, "We have all heard how Theseus killed the Minotaur . . . and how Actaeon saw Diana bathing naked and was set upon by his hounds for such gross impropriety."

Well, not anymore, in a time when popular culture rules. One wonders if Sigmund Freud were formulating his psychological theories in 2010, whether the famed Oedipus complex might not be replaced by an onanistic imperative. In this section, I highlight some words that hail from the vivid and lurid tales of mythology.

HALCYON

The word "halcyon" doesn't betray any connection to either our avian cousins or to tragedy, yet it is intrinsically connected with both. It is defined by *Webster's Third International Dictionary* as "pleasingly or idyllically calm or peaceful." The expression "halcyon days" refers to times of happiness and prosperity, yet this sense of calm prosperity also contains a storm. After a tempest had killed the husband of the wind goddess Alcyone, the bereft widow-goddess drowned herself in the sea. Punishing this suicide, the vengeful gods turned Alcyone and her husband Ceyx into birds later known as "halcyons," or kingfishers, as we call them today. Alcyone's "god-father" took pity on the couple and decreed that during the halcyons' mating season — the seven days before and after the shortest day of the year — the sea would be perfectly calm. This legend continued in the Roman era, when Alcyone became rendered as Halcyone, and endured well into the fifteenth century.

MONEY

It is common to locate the United States as the epicentre of our love of money and our obsession with the almighty dollar. Etymologically, however, we must cast the blame on the ancient Romans. "Money" derives from the Roman goddess Juno Moneta, who is literally "the Adviser," and also Jupiter's main squeeze. This name also applied to her temple in Rome, which contained a mint. So in due course, *moneta* came to mean "mint," then "stamp for coining" and finally "coin."

SYPHILIS

Outsiders are liable to be blamed for vice and immorality in our midst. Nothing better exemplifies this than the disease "syphilis." The Italians attributed it to the French and called it *Mal francese*. The French turned the tables and called it *Mal de Naples*. The Germans also targeted the French and labeled it *Franzosen böse Blattern*, "French bad blisters." The English called it "French pox," or the "French disease," and referred to the baldness that syphilis produced as a "French crown." To be "Frenchified" meant to have a venereal infection; a "French pig" was a venereal sore. The Russians blamed it on the Poles, who in turn called it the "German disease." In Dutch, it was rendered as *Spaensche Pokken*, "Spanish pox." Once the disease was transmitted eastward to India, Japan and China, it emerged as the "Portuguese disease" and, not surprisingly, Turks held Christians responsible. Finally, in the sixteenth century it received the more diplomatic designation "syphilis" that gained universal appeal. The name derives from a name of a fabled syphilitic shepherd in the poem *Syphilis sive Morbus Gallicus* by Italian poet Girolamo Fracastoro. This fable relates the story of the shepherd Syphilis whose blasphemy so angered the Sun God that he saddled poor Syphilis with an eponymous new disease. We read in a 1686 translation of Fracastoro's poem: "He first wore buboes dreadful to the sight, / First felt strange pains and sleepless pass'd the night."

Linguistic chauvinism dictates that not only is one's mother tongue "infected" by foreign influences, but that the alien languages are even responsible for the infections.

NEMESIS

The Greek goddess Nemesis was the goddess of retribution. She punished pretentiousness and hideous crimes with her sword and her avenging wings. Hence, "nemesis" has come to mean "an agent of retribution." Shakespeare used the word in *Henry VI, Part I* in 1591 but the first *OED* citation goes back to 1542. In the twentieth century its most common usage is as an arch-enemy or long-standing rival, e.g., Professor Moriarty to Sherlock Holmes or Rafael Nadal to Roger Federer.

CEREAL

In the fifth century BC, the Roman countryside was devastated by a severe drought. The priests consulted the local oracle who instructed them to adopt the new goddess Ceres (daughter of Saturn and Vesta) and make copious sacrifices in her honour. In exchange for these sacrifices, it became the mandate of Ceres to bring rain to the land and thus protect the crops. We get "cereal" from the Latin *cerealis* which means "of Ceres."

If Jupiter murdered Ceres, would that make him a cereal killer?

PANDER

In Greek mythology, Pandarus was an archer who led the Lycians in the Trojan War. He is presented as a heroic man who was honoured by his compatriots. In medieval accounts of the story of Troy, however, he is seen as a go-between in the ill-fated love affair between Troilus and Cressida. Because of this reputation, writers such as Chaucer and Shakespeare represented him in their stories as a pimp, a procurer who obtained the Trojan Cressida for the pleasure of Prince Troilus, the son of Priam, the Trojan king. "Pander" as a noun means "a pimp"; as a verb it means "to minister to the base appetites of others."

HYACINTH & NARCISSISM

The god Apollo accidentally killed the handsome Spartan lad Hyacinthus. He couldn't resuscitate him, so he did the next best thing and made a new flower spring from the red earth and called it a hyacinth. Yet another flower, the narcissus, was also born out of a homicide. The nymph Echo was unable to make the beautiful youth Narcissus fall in love with her, so she made him fall in love with himself, and he drowned while admiring his image in a still pool. After his death, the gods changed his body into a beautiful flower, the narcissus. A narcissus is linked etymologically to "narcotic," as it was believed that the flower possessed narcotic properties that could induce a state of torpor. "Narcissism," which refers to excessive self-love or vanity, was a neologism created by poet Samuel Taylor Coleridge in a letter that he wrote in 1822.

AMMONIA

Ultimately, "ammonia" comes from the Egyptian god of life and repro-
duction, Amon. Close to Amon's temple in Libya, archaeologists discovered deposits of ammonium chloride, called *sal ammoniac*, "salt of
Amon." It would appear that rather than worshipping at the temple,
some enterprising Bedouins extracted camel urine from the sand and
sold it as bleach for clothes. The gas nitrogen hydride derives from *sal
ammoniac*, and in 1782 Swedish chemist Torbern Bergman dubbed it
"ammonia." In common use today as a household cleaner, "ammonia"
is a solution of ammonia in water.

STENTORIAN

If you think your brother-in-law and Don Cherry are loudmouths, get
a load of Stentor. In the *Iliad*, Homer relates how this herald during the
Trojan War faced the enemy and announced terms in "a voice of fifty
men together." The word "stentorian" came into English in the early
part of the seventeenth century with the sense of "very loud and far-
reaching." It is curious that Homer should have named his bellowing
herald such, because in Greek *stenein* only means "moan" or "groan."

MENTOR

If you are going on a long journey and need to leave your home entrusted
to a friend, make sure that your choice is wiser than the one Odysseus
made when he embarked on his journey to the siege of Troy. He chose
his friend Mentor to protect his hearth and home, but Mentor was unable to stop rowdies from drinking his Bordeaux and single malts or
from butchering his cattle. The goddess Athene was watching the mayhem from Mount Olympus, and she decided to intervene by assuming
the body of Mentor and passing on some prudent advice to the son of
Odysseus, Telemachus, to put an end to this state of disorder. Hence, to
this day, "mentor" refers to a wise and trusted counsellor.

TEN WORDS
You Never Knew Were Related
to Death, Torture & Blood

Yea, death has always been with us so it is not surprising that it will have supplied words to our language, such as "euthanasia," from Greek, literally "good death," and "necrophiliac" (also from Greek), "lover of corpses." There are also many words in English that originally related to torture, which proves not only that *Homo sapiens* is a bloodthirsty species but also confirms that not all deaths are good deaths.

MORTGAGE

In days of yore when an impecunious noble heir had to borrow some quid for a new battle axe, chain mail or a faster steed, he would be compelled to sign a pledge to repay the debt when his father expired and the estate passed to him. "Mortgage" literally means "death pledge" as it marries the Old French *mort*, "death," and *gage*, "pledge." The depressing idea underlining this word is that if the mortgagor fails to repay the loan, the property pledged as security is lost, or "dead," to him or her.

Interestingly, although "mortgage" derives from French, the present French word for it is *hypotheque*. Two other "mort" words that are death-related are "amortize" and "mortify." While to amortize a debt is to gradually pay it off or extinguish it, the word was first used by Chaucer in 1386 to refer to the killing of sin. The first sense of "mortify" appeared in John Wycliffe's translation of the Bible in 1382 and meant "to put to death." Today it is more commonly used to suggest humiliation or extreme embarrassment.

Notwithstanding my morbid analysis of the etymology of the word "mortgage," or the recent collapse of the housing market, please don't be loath to obtain a mortgage on your house. Just make sure it's not a mortifying one.

CRONE

Although no one would think a crone describes an attractive person, its etymology suggests an even more gruesome, macabre individual. The word derives from the Middle Dutch *caroonje*, or *croonje*, "carcass," which bequeathed the French *carogne*, "carcass," and the English "carrion." Confirming the sexist nature of language, the *OED* notes, "Rarely applied to a worn-out old man."

TRAVEL

The first definition of "travel" in the *OED* is "Labour, toil; suffering, trouble," and if you think this puts a damper on travel, a further investigation of the word only makes the journey more torturous. The word ultimately descends from the Latin *trepalium*, a three-pointed stake used to torture prisoners by the Church in the sixth century. In any case, fear of the *trepalium* must have served as an incentive to work harder, because the French took this word and Frenchified it as *travail*, the word for "work." When English borrowed this word from French in the fourteenth century it meant several things such as "work," "being in labour," and "travel." Travel in the Middle Ages was generally an arduous task and was undertaken only when absolutely necessary or by those engaging in a pilgrimage that might mend the soul while wreaking havoc on the body. Thus when beginners of French mistranslate the verb *travailler* (meaning "to work") as "to travel" (because of its similar look), they are not so far off as their teachers might suggest. When we say "farewell" we are really wishing "travel well," lest we be overrun by brigands or some other calamity befall us on our trek.

ORDEAL

The word "ordeal" was usually found in the phrase "trial by ordeal" and it reflects a legal practice found in medieval British courts. The *OED* states, "In Anglo-Saxon and Norman England, until its abolition in 1215, the ordeal could take any of four forms: fire, hot water, cold water, and trial by combat." As in modern-day reality shows, these ordeals were somewhat rigged. To be declared innocent one would have to accomplish the impossible, such as carrying red-hot coals without being burned. Similarly, in the sixteenth and seventeenth centuries witches were judged innocent if they sank when placed in the local pond, and guilty if they floated (and then condemned to death). It was only in the seventeenth century that "ordeal" acquired its metaphorical and less painful meaning of a "trying experience."

BLESS

Picture this scene. Someone unleashes a hearty sneeze, and being properly reared you counter "Bless you." You then notice that the sneezer's nose is bleeding. This makes proper etymological sense as the Anglo-Saxon *blóedsian*, "to consecrate" came from the Germanic root *blód*, "blood." Over the centuries, the spelling of *blóedsian* transformed to "blescen," then "blessen" and eventually to "bless." We see the blood connection in French with the verb *blesser*, which means "to wound."

With the advent of Christianity in Britain, *blóedsian* was used to translate the Latin *benedicere*, "to consecrate by religious ritual." According to the *OED*, the verb originally meant "to make 'sacred' or 'holy' with blood; to consecrate by some sacrificial rite which was held to render a thing inviolable from profane use of men and evil influence of men or demons." Hopefully, the sneeze exorcized the demons.

ROUÉ

This word for a debauched person comes from the French *rouer*, "to break on the wheel." You would definitely not want to be on this particular wheel as it was an instrument of torture likely to elicit confessions by mutilating its spinning victims. The name was first given to the profligate companions of the Duke of Orleans, circa 1720, to suggest that their lives of debauchery rendered them deserving of this extreme punishment.

CRUCIAL

We get "crucial" from the Latin word for "cross," *crux*. Actually, *crux* didn't signify only a cross but other "excruciating" (which also derives from *crux*) forms of torture, including the stake, or the gibbet — a form of gallows where the bodies of criminals were hung in chains after execution. In anatomy, "crucial" means cross-shaped, and thus we have "crucial incision." It also refers to the name of two ligaments in the knee-joint, which cross each other in the form of the letter X, and connect the tibia and femur. In the seventeenth century the word came to refer to something that decides between two rival hypotheses, proving the one and disproving the other, and thus we have our current meaning of something critically or crucially important.

PLETHORA

This word first surfaced in the sixteenth century at which time the sense was medical and referred to an overabundance of blood or other bodily fluids. By the middle of the seventeenth century, the more general sense of "surplus" became the dominant meaning, most often with a negative sense. In current usage, the negative quality has dropped out, and we are left with "plethora" meaning "a very large amount."

SMIRCH

This word was used by Shakespeare to mean "stain" or "smear," and in the nineteenth century to mean "discredit." Its first sense in 1495 of "make dirty" does not give us a hint of the word's etymology as it derives from the Old French *esmorcher*, "to torment or torture," by the application of hot metal.

TANTALIZING

The word "tantalizing" in its meaning of "tempting" doesn't hint at the agonizing torment of its hero, Tantalus. He was the son of Zeus and he made the mistake of divulging the secret of the gods to humanity. For this defiance of the Olympian code of *omerta*, he was plunged into a pool of water in Hades, with a succulent fruit tree just above his head. Whenever he tried to drink the water or eat the fruit, they moved away from him, causing him unbearable thirst and hunger. This etymology might make you reconsider ordering those "tantalizing lobsters" advertized at your local fish market.

TEN WORDS
You Never Knew Came
from Our Vices

⌒

In this section, which could be subtitled *Booze, Gamble & Get Naked*, I look at words that have sordid associations with activities considered as no-no's by some incorruptible members of society.

AMETHYST

What is your favourite cure for a hangover? Aspirin? cold pizza? vitamin C? coffee? Vegemite on toast? another beer? The ancient Greeks also couldn't agree on the best remedy, but one of their charms against drunkenness was the stone *amethystos*, which blends *a*, "not," with *methystos*, "drunk," and provided the English word "amethyst." It was originally spelled "amatist" (as in *amo, amas, amat*) but rest assured that etymologically speaking it has nothing to do with love. In any case, I think I'll stick with extra-strength Tylenol after an excess of revelling.

HAZARD

The *OED* relates that going back to the twelfth century, a "hazard" referred to "a game at dice in which the chances are complicated by a number of arbitrary rules." As the cast of the dice is mere chance, the word eventually acquired the meaning an "unforeseen accident." This game is mentioned by Chaucer's louche Pardoner in *The Canterbury Tales* who likens its corrupting influence on youth to brothels. Ultimately, the word descends from the Arabic, *al-zahr*, "luck." For links enthusiasts, I can relate that its first golfing usage transcends Tiger Woods' peccadilloes by approximately 150 years and is found in 1857 from *Chambers' Information*: "He possibly drives his ball into some hazard — such as sand or whin . . . from which he is only extricated after expending several strokes in the operation." In case you are wondering, "whin" is furze or gorse, a type of shrub. (I had to look it up, too).

𝒪𝓀 WED

With the divorce rate as high as it is and with divorce lawyers lurking like carrion-seeking vultures, I don't regard it as overly harsh to assert that marriage is a bit of a risk. Etymologically, it is also a gamble, as originally in the twelfth century the word referred to "wager," or something deposited as a security, and only took on its nuptial sense two centuries later.

𝒪𝓀 BRIDAL

If being in a bridal party drives you to drink, it just might relate to the word's etymology. You should, however, not be sipping champagne, but rather guzzling ale, as "bridal" weds the Old English words *bryd*, "bride" with *eaou*, "ale." There is a reference to the libation *bryd ealo* in the *Old English Chronicles* of 1075.

𝒪𝓀 LAMPOON

This word comes from French, and the *OED* states, "French etymologists regard the noun 'lampoon' as from *lampons*, 'let us drink', imperative of *lamper* (slang) to booze, guzzle." It seems that *lampe*, in turn, came from *laper*, an onomatopoeic word suggested the lapping of water. In sixteenth-century France it was not unusual for satirical songs to be embellished with the refrain *Lampons!* and when the word "lampoon" was first used in English in the seventeenth century its sense was of a vitriolic satire unleashed against an opponent. Since that time, the sense of vitriol in the word has lessened.

SYMPOSIUM

If you are cynical by nature and believe that many symposia are an excuse to become sozzled, you have etymology in your corner. The word blends the Greek prefix *syn-*, "together," and the Greek word *pino*, "drink." The ancient Greeks held their symposia after dinner where intellectual entertainment shared the spotlight with drinking wine. By the eighteenth century the word came to refer to a meeting or conference for discussion of some subject, where the imbibing of copious amounts of wine, although encouraged, was not mandatory.

GYMNASIUM

In the unlikely event that you are asked to strip naked in a gym by a philologist — don't panic. It might be because of his/her awareness that the Greek word *gumnos* means "naked." It was customary for athletes in ancient Greece to train as the gods — or whoever created them — in the buff. Hence, the verb *gumndzein* came to mean "train" or "practice." This semantic process gave rise to the noun *gumnasion* that the Latin tongue borrowed as *gymnasium*, "school." In German-speaking countries the academic sense of the word — a school — remains, whereas English has opted for the original athletic meaning.

ABSTEMIOUS

Remember your first shot of whisky? If your experience resembles mine, I wouldn't be surprised if it caused a choking sensation in your throat. If we go far back in time, we find that in Sanskrit *tam* meant "to choke," and the word "abstemious" blends the Greek *abs* "away from" with *teme-tum*, "intoxicating liquor." Hence, the *tem/tam* part of the word advises one to stay "away from" liquor, lest it compress your throat. The *OED* informs us that to be abstemious means to dispense with "wine and rich food." Etymologically speaking, however, you can still enjoy your foie gras.

CALLOW

One only hears the word "callow" nowadays in the sense of "inexperienced" and usually modifying the noun "youth," but the word originally meant "bare" in the sense of being bald or beardless. Alexander Tulloch, in *Word Routes* mentions that this word is related to the Russian word for "naked," *goliy*. Perhaps, but it also seems to stem from young birds which did not yet have their feathers, as in the quotation from Holland's *Plutarch* of 1603: "Yoong callow birds which are not yet fethered and fledg'd."

BEVY

The Latin verb "to drink" is *bibere*, which bequeathed the Italian *bevuta* "drinking-bout, a draught" and *beva* "drink, liquor, potion." *Bevee* came into Old English with the meaning of a "group of drinkers." The *OED* states that "To explain the English sense, it has been conjectured that *bevy* may have passed from the sense of 'drinking-bout' to 'drinking-party,' and to 'party' or 'company' generally." It also indicates that it is "the proper term for a company of maidens or ladies, of roes, of quails, or of larks" — a great distance from drinking and drinkers.

TEN WORDS
You Never Knew Came
from People's Names

I concur with this pearl from Woody Allen: "I don't want to gain immortality through my work, I want to gain immortality by not dying."

Unfortunately, for those of us who aren't convinced that there is life after death, the only way of achieving immortality is by passing on your genes to the next generation or by being an eponym. You can have a comet named after you, which was the method used by Alan Hale, or a disease, which was the technique employed by Dr. James Parkinson. Alternatively, your ideas can be highlighted, as in such words as Freudian, Machiavellian and Christian. In this section, I look at people who have bequeathed their names to words but who, unfortunately, have not received due recognition.

﹏ DUNCE

There is a Spanish proverb that states, "Unless a fool knows Latin, he is not a great fool." Thirteenth-century John Duns Scotus' defence of the doctrine of the Immaculate Conception earned him the title Doctor Subtilis, so I suppose that he qualifies as a great fool. Ironically, this brilliant scholar's name also provided us with the term "dunce." The term "Duns men" or "dunces" was originally applied in the early part of the sixteenth century to those who were believed to engage in what they regarded as the hair-splitting sophistry of Duns Scotus. Such philosophers were referred to as "the Dunce-men and Sophisters." However, by the end of the century the word started to be used to refer to a dull-witted, stupid person. The cartoon character sitting in the corner with a conical hat marked with a "D" is a long way from the great Duns Scotus who argued that existence itself is our most abstract and fundamental concept.

✒ MAVERICK

While the term "maverick" nowadays is often associated with the Republican team of John McCain and Sarah Palin, we have to go back to nineteenth-century south Texas to find the progenitor of this term. Samuel Augustus Maverick was a lawyer and politician, and happenstance cattleman. It transpired that a client gave him several hundred cattle to settle a debt, and as Maverick didn't particularly care for tending cattle, he left them in the care of others. These cattle were never branded and were allowed to roam freely, and as a result some unscrupulous cattlemen seized the cattle, branded them and claimed them as their own. Hence, by 1867 the term "maverick" referred to an un-branded calf. By the 1880s the term came to refer to a politician whose heart, soul and mind were not owned by a political party and more generally to an unorthodox or independent-minded individual. Ironically, considering "maverick" is nowadays associated with the aforementioned right-wing politicians, several of Samuel Maverick's heirs have been actively involved in liberal causes. In October 2008, Terrelita Maverick, a member of the American Civil Liberty Union, stated, "It's just incredible . . . to suggest that he [John McCain] is not part of that Republican herd. . . . He's branded."

~ LEOTARD

For some peculiar reason I can't discern, many English words are named after French people. Observe the following words that come from Gallic personages: "chauvinist," "guillotine," "begonia," "nicotine," "pompadour," "ampere" and "leotard." "Leotard" owes its name to nineteenth-century French trapezist Jules Léotard. Being dissatisfied with the cumbersome outfits available to aerialists of his era, Léotard designed his own costume, the snug one-piece elastic garment that bears his name to this day and is first recorded in 1920. His aerodynamic motives may not have been entirely pure, for in his *Memoires de Léotard* he asks rhetorically, "Do you want to be adored by the ladies? . . . Then put on a more natural garb, which does not hide your best features."

~ BOYCOTT

This word sprang into use in 1880 to describe the activities of the Irish Land League. This organization had been set up some years before to press for agrarian reforms in Ireland. Those who objected to their aims were subjected to an ostracization process. One of the first to suffer this fate was an estate manager named Captain Charles Cunningham Boycott. In a November 1880 article, the London *Times* employed the word "boycott" as a verb and the next month as a noun. For politically correct folks who find the word "boycott" somewhat sexist, I'm happy to announce that as of March 2008, the word "girlcott" appeared in the *OED* with the definition, "A boycott carried out by a woman or group of women."

~ CHAUVINISM

We owe this word to nineteenth-century French soldier Nicolas Chauvin whose excessive patriotism, while originally celebrated, eventually came to be ridiculed by his comrades. After Napoleon suffered his Waterloo, the term was applied mockingly to old soldiers of the Empire, who professed a sort of idolatrous admiration for the accomplishments of the

Little Corporal. By the middle of the twentieth century, the word chauvinism was extended to any group that shows partiality or excessive attachment to a cause, and by 1970 the dominant sense of the word was in the phrase "male chauvinist," with a three-letter (non-kosher) word frequently added.

GUY

The original guy was Guy Fawkes, who in 1605 perpetrated the Gunpowder Plot that would have blown up the British Houses of Parliament — had it succeeded. The failure of this plot is celebrated in England on November 5, and is known as Guy Fawkes Day. It is traditional during the celebration to burn effigies of Mr. Fawkes. By the turn of the nineteenth century these effigies became known as "guys." Later the term was applied to any person of grotesque appearance, and in 1847, probably as a result of the carousing that occurred on Guy Fawkes Day, the term "guy" came to be used to refer to any man — both bad guys and good guys. Since the 1980s "guys" is increasingly used to refer to women as well as men, particularly in mixed groups of both sexes, although many women resent the term as being low-class.

SILHOUETTE

French author and politician Étienne de Silhouette was a finance minister in the late 1750s who gained a reputation for parsimony. Consequently, the word "silhouette" came to be applied to anything skimped. One account of the application of the word to a "simple cut-out picture" states that it carries a notion of simplicity, but another theory posits that Monsieur Silhouette himself was in the habit of making such pictures. The first use of the word in this context is in 1798 in the *Monthly Review*; by the middle of the nineteenth century the metaphorical sense of a "dark image against a bright background" had developed. By 1875 it was employed in this sense as a verb. A most useful word to have been developed from someone known for being cheap.

LYNCH

This verb for extra-juridical punishment owes its existence to William Lynch, a planter and justice of the peace in Virginia who at the beginning of the nineteenth century took it upon himself to set up unofficial tribunals to try suspects. His brand of justice was dubbed Lynch's law and later lynch law. Its first citation as a verb is in 1836. While lynchings were performed both on blacks and whites, it was usually reserved for blacks in the American South who were not protected by laws as whites were. It is estimated that between 1880 and 1960 at least 3,500 African Americans were lynched in the United States.

GALVANIZE

This word derives from the eighteenth-century Italian scientist Luigi Galvani, whose research led to the discovery that electricity can result from chemical action. The noun "galvanism" and the adjective "galvanic" are first recorded in 1797; the verb "galvanize" surfaces in 1802. By the middle of the nineteenth century the verb acquired a metaphorical sense of stimulating a person or a group into action. When Charlotte Bronte in *Villette* writes of how "her approach always galvanized him to new and spasmodic life," one has the picture of the poor man in spasms, twitching like one of Galvani's frogs.

GARDENIA

One would assume "gardenia" comes from the word "garden." Indirectly it does, but more precisely it derives from the name of a gardener called Alexander Garden, a noted botanist of South Carolina. In his honour, a whole genus of tropical trees and shrubs was named Gardenia in 1760 by classifying botanist Carolus Linnaeus. One wonders if Americans are pleased with this acclaim, for when the American Revolution began, Garden sided with the Brits and at the end of the war he left America and never returned.

PART II
Strange & Exotic
Bedfellows of English

TEN WORDS
You Never Knew Came
from French

I can't decide if I'm amused or bemused when I read an article about "the rape of German by English," "the assault of anglicisms in Poland," or the alleged fact that "French is being deluged by English." If ever there was a language that has been inundated by other languages, it is English. French is by far the worst assailant. *Mon dieu, sacre bleu, zut alors;* we're not even a Romance language and we must endure so many galling Gallicisms! Truth be known, there are more English words that derive from French than from the original Anglo-Saxon word stock. But although English seems to prefer borrowing words from French over all other languages, it has taken some words from virtually every tongue on our planet. Educator Joseph Bellafiore describes English as a "lagoon of nations" because its vocabulary contains thousands of words "floating like ships from foreign ports freighted with messages for us." English didn't get to be the global language by being pure, and in this section we will look at "corruptions" from several languages. You might be somewhat shocked to discover the actual linguistic paternity of some words.

After the Norman Invasion of 1066, the English language imported countless words from French and, in the process, hundreds of Old English words disappeared from the language. In fact, no more than 20 percent of Old English words have descendants today. Words that relate to the government, administration or religious authority are almost exclusively French in origin. Observe "government," "administration," "country," "court," "royal," "crown," "state," "castle," "judge," "sacrament," and "grace" to name but a few. Similarly, the domain of dining is also French-dominated, with English absorbing from French such basic words as "soup," "salad," "lettuce," "poultry," "fruit" and "dessert."

Even twentieth-century English has been "tainted" with Gallicisms such as "chauffeur," "brassiere," "aileron" and "détente." It is time to admit that our beloved mother tongue is essentially poorly pronounced French.

Usually, the French pedigree of words is readily apparent. But sometimes words mutate to such an extent on their voyage into our language as to obscure the connection. In this chapter, we'll look at some words whose French pedigree is not apparent. As a case in point, we'll start with that very word "pedigree."

PEDIGREE

If you take pride in your pedigree, you might be humbled to know that, etymologically speaking, you are crowing about the "foot of a crane," *pied de grue*. Old documents that recorded a family tree used a three-line graph that apparently resembled the imprint of the bony foot of the crane. Some of the early spellings of "pedigree" include "pedicru," "pee de grewe," "petegreu," and "peedegre." By the eighteenth century, "pedigree" became the accepted form. It's ironic that the word "pedigree," so associated with pure-bred animals, is a highly mutated word. *C'est la vie des mots*.

BELFRY

A belfry is a bell tower, so naturally the word is connected etymologically with "bell." Right? Wrong. In twelfth-century France, a *berfroi* was
a wooden siege tower that could be moved up against the walls of a castle when it was being attacked. Apparently the *berfroi* was in the beginning just a small wooden defensive structure to protect the besiegers,
but as it grew in height it took on the shape of a bell tower, and by the
sixteenth century this was rendered in English as "belfroy" or "belfry."

BUDGET

French merchants of the Middle Ages carried their money around in a
bougette, "small bag" or "wallet." English borrowed this word as *bow-
gette* in the sixteenth century and by 1611 had settled on the spelling
"budget." By the end of the seventeenth century, the word was being
used to refer to the contents of a wallet. By 1733, the financial sense of
"budget" emerged when Sir Robert Walpole, first minister (*de facto*
prime minister), introduced an unpopular excise duties bill. A political
pamphleteer immediately attacked Walpole in a pamphlet entitled *The
Budget Opened*, comparing him to "a mountebank opening his budget
of quack medicines and conjuring tricks." The pamphleteer went on to
ask rhetorically how the "budget" was to be opened, and answered,
"Why by an Alteration only of the present Method of collecting the
publick Revenues. . . . So then, out it comes at last. The Budget is
opened; and our State Emperick hath dispensed his packets by his Zany
Couriers through all Parts of the Kingdom. . . . I do not pretend to
understand this Art of political Legerdemain." In this example, one can
watch how, in the very act of satire, the idea of "budget," referring to a
bag, is in the process of becoming the contents of the bag. The satiric
use of the word "budget" disappeared within a few short years, leaving
us with our present meaning of the "estimate of revenue and expenditure." The notion of "Zany Couriers" dispensing the "packets" of loot,
however, has not entirely disappeared.

ॐ CURFEW

If you establish a curfew for a teenager, you may be doing so to protect the young hellion from metaphorical burns. A curfew, however, was established originally not to avoid metaphorical fires but actual ones. In medieval Europe, it was not uncommon for a town to ring a bell at a fixed hour in the evening, signalling that street fires be extinguished, sometimes by covering the fire. This applied also to lights and was termed *couvre feu*, French for "cover fire." This morphed almost immediately in English to "curfew," and by the thirteenth century "curfew" merely designated the time the evening bell was rung. Only in the twentieth century was the sense of "curfew" extended to refer to other restricted outdoor nocturnal activities. *Punch* magazine in 1939 remarked on "the attempt . . . to get a nine o'clock curfew imposed on members of the Women's Land Army in training . . . to prevent them going out with soldiers." How ironic that a French word should dampen passion!

ॐ GOPHER

The *OED* sports this notation for its entry "gopher": "According to *Webster* 1848–64, *gaufre* was used by the French settlers in North America as a name for various burrowing animals, and is a transferred use of *gaufre*, honeycomb." Hence, the gopher honeycombs, i.e., digs a hole for its burrow. Not to be confused with the gopher wood ostensibly used for Noah's ark or with "gofer," the person who runs errands, sometimes referred to as a "dog's body" — so perhaps not all that different after all from the little burrowing animal who disappears into the ground.

ॐ JEOPARDY

Jeu parti was originally a French chess term meaning "game divided." When a game is equally divided, both players are in danger of losing and for this reason *jeu parti* came to mean "uncertainty" and eventually to refer to "serious danger." Its first English usage "ieupardyes" comes from Chaucer in 1369 in *The Dethe of Blaunche the Duchesse*. The spelling "jeopardy" became standard only in the second half of the seventeenth century. Today it is also the name of a popular television game show.

PIONEER

A "pioneer" is thought of as someone who paves the way for others, and indeed the word comes from the Old French, *peonier*, "foot soldier," who would prepare the way for other soldiers. The *OED*'s first definition of the word in 1523 bears this military connection: "One of a body of foot-soldiers who march with . . . an army or regiment, having spades, pickaxes etc., to dig trenches, repair roads and perform other labours in clearing and preparing the way for the main body." By 1572 the word "pioneer" was being used to describe an early settler, but Shakespeare has the military sense in mind in the following passage from *Othello*: "I had been happy that the general camp, / Pioners and all, had tasted her sweet body." In various Communist countries after World War I, this sense of an advance party was captured in the name of an organization for children to advance Communist ideals.

PUNY

The word "puny" is a phonetic spelling of the twelfth-century French *puisne*, from *puis*, "later" and *né*, "born." The word "puisne" (pronounced as "puny") still exists in English with the specific designation in law to refer to a judge of a lower rank. The sense that "puny" suggests weakness derives from the fact that younger children have less strength than older ones. The old Charles Atlas ads used to picture "puny" men who needed the bodybuilding courses to respond to bullies who kicked sand in their faces.

◢ VAUDEVILLE

The term "vaudeville" is actually a bastardization of *vau de Vire*, "valley of Vire," Vire being the capital of Calvados, in Normandy. *Les chansons du Vau de Vire* were drinking songs, first created in the fifteenth century, that often satirized local personalities. Originally, the word "vaudeville" was used in English to refer to a "popular song"; the sense of "light variety entertainment" emerged at the beginning of the nineteenth century.

◢ ZYDECO

This term refers to a kind of dance music that originated in southern Louisiana that marries blues with Cajun influence; it is performed on an accordion, guitar or violin. "Zydeco" appears to be a total bastardization of *les haricots* ("the beans") that appears in the dance tune title *Les haricots sont pas sales (The beans are not dirty)*. Both the fields of music and dancing are prone to adopt descriptive food terms. Observe jam, salsa, hambone, hoecake, chops, and former jazz great Jellyroll Morton and his Red Hot Peppers studio band.

TEN WORDS
You Never Knew Came from
Yiddish/Hebrew

In recent years, English has been overrun by Yiddishisms such as "schmuck," "kibitz," "bagel," "chutzpah," "shlep" and "verklempt." By and large, people are aware of the Yiddish lineage of these words. There are also many words in English with religious senses, such as "rabbi," "amen," "kosher," "hallelujah" and "Armageddon," that have a clear Hebrew pedigree. Yet there are many words in English that enjoy Hebrew and Yiddish roots that most people, including Jews, are not aware of. Go figure. Who knew? Of course, what qualifies as a word with Jewish lineage is sometimes as contentious as who qualifies as a Jew.

Here are some of the words that surprisingly seem to bear a Jewish heritage.

KIBOSH

The *OED* has this rather terse, tepid comment about the word's origin: "It has been stated to be Yiddish or Anglo-Hebraic." This is the most popular source, though the details differ. One supposition claims the word comes from the Yiddish word *kabas* or *kabbasten*, "to suppress." Another view is odder, claiming that it is an acronym formed from the initial letters of three Yiddish words meaning "eighteen British coins": the Hebrew *chai* for "eighteen," and *shekel*, meaning "coin," with "British" in the middle. But, as Leo Rosten argues, that ought to make *kibrosh* rather than *kibosh*. Rosten states, however, that there was special significance in the number eighteen, since in Gematria (an important method of divination among Jews at one time), this was the number equivalent to the word "life."

Whatever its origin, most authorities seem to agree that the word first appeared in Britain in the early part of the nineteenth century. The *OED* seems to agree and cites Charles Dickens' *Sketches by Boz* written in 1836 as the first use in print. In any case, "kibosh" soon made the transatlantic schlep to the United States and became a popular slang word to describe "doing someone in." Early written references varied a lot in spelling. Dickens spelled it "kye-bosk" (presumably a literal spelling of the then Cockney pronunciation); the London humour magazine *Punch* used "cibosh" in an article in 1856 and the modern spelling "kibosh" appeared first in *The Slang Dictionary* in 1869.

Not all etymologists, however, are convinced of the Jewish heritage of "kibosh." It is said by some to have a heraldic origin, being derived from *caboshed* which is the description of the emblem of an animal which is shown full-face, but cut off close to the ears so that no neck appears. Another theory argues that the word originates in the Gaelic phrase *cie báis* meaning "cap of death." The word *báis* is apparently pronounced "bawsh" and *cie* is pronounced with a hard initial consonant, somewhat like "kai."

Perhaps one day an etymologist will find an earlier citation for the word that definitively ties down the origin to one of these explanations, and we will at long last put the kibosh on this debate.

GLITCH

Many sources, including the *Random House Historical Dictionary*, state that "glitch" comes from the German *glitschen* and/or from the Yiddish *gletshn* meaning "to slip." The *OED* lists its etymology as "unknown," but its first citation in 1962 from astronaut John Glenn's book *Into Orbit* confirms a NASA connection: "Another term we adopted to describe some of our problems was 'glitch.' Literally, a glitch is a spike or change in voltage in an electrical circuit which takes place when the circuit suddenly has a new load put on it. . . . A glitch . . . is such a minute change in voltage that no fuse could protect against it." Today it is used generally to refer to a hitch or a snag in a planned activity. In Yiddish we also find the delightful, onomatopoeic adjective *glitchidik*, "slippery."

BROUHAHA

Some etymological theories, while not necessarily entrenched, are so interesting that it is worthwhile relating them. *Webster's Dictionary of Word Origins* provides one of these. It says that the word "brouhaha" comes from the Hebrew phrase *barukh habba*, "blessed is he who enters," that is found in Psalm 118. To support the Hebrew etymology, *Webster's* points out that the Italian dialect words *barucaba* and *badonai* (from Hebrew *be adonai*, "by God") mean "hubbub." The intent of these words, according to *Webster's*, was to mock Jews who were seen by some Italians as a diabolical presence. *Webster's* also offers a less spicy theory of Hebrew origin. Because the expression *barukh habba* was often uttered in a mechanical fashion without knowledge of its meaning, it could have come to mean "meaningless speech" in the same manner that "patter" derives from *Pater Noster*. Although the *Barnhart Concise Dictionary of Etymology* is not as forceful as *Webster's* in promoting the Hebrew etymology, it does allow that it is a possibility.

❧ JOT

We read in the King James Bible in Matthew 5:18, "Till heaven and earth pass, one jot or one tittle shall in no wise pass from the law, till all be fulfilled." Earlier, in 1526, William Tyndale, whose translation was often the basis for the King James version, had used "jot" in the same passage from Matthew. This word comes from the Greek and Latin *iota*, but ultimately from *yodh*, the smallest letter in the Hebrew alphabet.

❧ CINNAMON

The *OED* states that the word "cinnamon" can be traced from Latin back to Greek and ultimately to the Hebrew word *qinnāmôn*. The word *qinnāmôn* is used in Exodus 30:23, when Moses is commanded to use both sweet cinnamon and cassia. Later in Proverbs 7:17, we read where the lover's bed is perfumed with myrrh and cinnamon; and in the Song of Solomon 4:14, the beauty of a lover is likened to cinnamon scent.

Notwithstanding this evidence, the *Brown-Driver-Briggs-Gesenius Hebrew-English Lexicon* (*BDBGHEL*) disagrees, and believes it is likely that "cinnamon" comes from Malay. In Malay, "cinnamon" is rendered as *kayu manis* or *kainamanis*, which literally means "sweet wood." *BDBGHEL* points out that two of the three biblical references to *qinnāmôn* are attributed to King Solomon who had the financial means to import exotic spices.

❧ CIDER

Ultimately, "cider" comes from the Hebrew *shekar*, "intoxicating liquor" or "strong drink." In John Wycliffe's 1382 translation of the Bible, he offers us this passage in Judges 13:4, "Be war thanne, lest thou drynke wyn and sither." Until the seventeenth century, "sicar" was the most common rendering of the word. The word "shicker" to mean "intoxicated" is found not only in Jewish speech but has also filtered into English, as it is used in Australia and New Zealand. Today the word generally refers to a drink made from apple juice that is fermented (especially in the west country of England), although in the United States it often describes merely plain apple juice, unfermented.

BEHEMOTH

We read in Job 40:10 of a behemoth that most observers believe was a hippopotamus. The word first appears in 1382 in John Wycliffe's translation of the Bible. In form, the word is the plural of *behamah*, "beast," and it may ultimately come from the Egyptian *pehemau*, "water ox." Today one encounters the word only occasionally to indicate something huge, perhaps a tank.

SAPPHIRE

We know that this stone was rendered in ancient Hebrew as *sappir*. Some etymologists believe, however, that the Hebrew word came from the Sanskrit, *sanipriya*, which means literally "dear to the planet Saturn." Cheesy novels will sometimes have their heroes with eyes of "sapphire blue."

CABAL

People like to attribute acronymic origins to words, and there are some wonderful acronymic myths for word origins such as "fuck" standing for "Fornication Under Consent of King," or "golf" deriving from "Gentlemen Only, Ladies Forbidden." There is also a folk etymology that the word "cabal" derives from the names of Clifford, Arlington, Buckingham, Ashley and Lauderdale, who served as ministers and formed an inner circle in the government of Charles II in the seventeenth century.

A "cabal" is a group of plotters, or a secret plot itself, and while this sense emerged during the reign of Charles II, the word was not developed as a mnemonic device to remember his conniving ministerial staff. The word ultimately can be traced back to "cabbala" that comes from the Hebrew *qabbalah*, "tradition." The *OED* defines "cabbala" as "The name given in post-biblical Hebrew to the oral tradition handed down from Moses to the Rabbis of the Mishnah and the Talmud." It was during the Middle Ages that secret meetings of groups steeped in the arcane mysteries of the cabbala gave rise to the English word "cabal." In England, Gordon Brown has been the intended victim of many cabals. And if Barack Obama continues in his present direction it is likely that he too will soon be another cabal victim.

ABRACADABRA

Etymologists are not certain about the origin of this magical word. One theory holds that it ultimately comes from the Hebrew *berakah* and *dabar*, "blessing" and "speech," or from an unknown Aramaic word for a demon. It is first mentioned in the second century AD in a poem by Quintus Severus Sammonicus. According to Robert Hendrickson, in *Word and Phrase Origins*, the word was "believed to be a charm with the power to cure toothaches, fevers, and other ills, especially if written on parchment in a triangular arrangement and suspended from the neck by a linen thread." By the way, I tried this cure to ease my sore back and it didn't work, but possibly my arrangement of parchment was not sufficiently triangular.

TEN WORDS
You Never Knew Came
from Arabic

The *OED* contains over 1,000 words that derive from Arabic. While there are many words that one would expect to be of Arabic origin such as "harem," "mosque," "sheik," "fatwa" and "jihad," there are many other common English words of Arabic lineage that will surprise you. It is obvious that the Iraqi prison Abu Ghraib (literally, "father of little crows") is Arabic; not as apparent is the Arabic lineage of Alcatraz (the full account of which is to be found in the final section). Ultimately, it derives from *al-qadus*, the Arabic term for a bucket as part of a water-raising irrigation wheel.

In this chapter, I look at ten serendipitous words of Arabic lineage.

ALCOHOL

That ancient exotic Levantine trio of Cleopatra, Nefertiti and the Queen of Sheba probably applied an antimony paste to their eyelids called *al-kuhl*, the *al* part meaning "the" and the *kuhl* ending meaning "powdered antimony." Arab alchemists gave the name of *al-kuhl* to any finely pulverized powder obtained by sublimation and thus to all compounds obtained through the distillation process. The word first came into English as "alcool," and this referred to any fine powder. The first *OED* citation is from George Sandys' *Travels* in 1615: "They put betweene the eye-lids and the eye a certaine black powder . . . made of a minerall brought from the kingdome of Fez, and called Alcohole." Given the Islamic prohibition against drinking alcohol, it is ironic that this word derives from Arabic. However, it was not until the nineteenth century that the word "alcohol" became used exclusively to denote the West's favourite liquid.

ALGEBRA

This word derives from the Arabic *al-jebr* which means "the reuniting of broken parts." When "algebra" first entered the English language it referred to the setting of broken bones, and sometimes to the fractures themselves. A faithful Arabic rendering of what we call "algebra" is *ilm al-jebr wa'l muqabalah*, and it means "reduction and comparison by equations." As late as 1623 we find an *OED* citation that only refers to "algebra" as "bone-setting."

ASSASSIN

This word literally means "hashish-eater," (the Arabic word is *hashshash*) and it entered our lexicon in 1237. The *OED* offers the following partial quotation: "certain Muslim fanatics, in the time of the Crusades, who were sent forth by their sheik, 'the old man of the mountain,' to murder the Christian leaders. . . ." These executions were committed under the influence of hashish, so it is safe to assume that the use of hashish was at least deleterious to the health of the Crusaders being attacked. In virtually all European languages a word such as *assassin* in French or *asesino* in Spanish came to be applied to one who murders for political and religious rather than personal motives.

MAGAZINE

The word "magazine" ultimately derives from the Arabic *makhāzin*, the plural of *makhzan*, "storehouse." The word was rendered in Spanish as *almagagen* and entered English via the French *magasin* and Italian *magazzino* in the fourteenth century. Its first sense in the *OED* is "a place where goods are laid up; a storehouse for goods," and this sense of storing lives on in its ammunition meaning: a gun's magazine as a holder of bullets or cartridges. Its sense as a periodical emerged almost accidentally in 1731 when the editors of the *Gentleman's Magazine* used this word because they said that they intended "to treasure up, as in a Magazine, the most remarkable Pieces." The term, however, caught on almost immediately to refer to a periodical publication and this became the dominant sense of the word.

ADMIRAL

An admiral, etymologically, doesn't command the seas. The word derives from the Arabic *amir* "commander," from which English also acquired the word "emir." A commander of the sea is *amir-al-bahr*; a commander of the faithful is rendered as *amir-al-muminin*. Sailors from the West assumed that *amiral* was one word and they gleaned that it designated a title of respect. By the early thirteenth century the word was used by English seamen to mean "commander of." Some of the early spellings included "amrayl," "amyrayl," as well as "admirale" and "admiral."

COFFEE

In *Word Origins* by Wilfred Funk, we read about a legend of a goatherd named Kaldi who lived in the Arabian Peninsula in the ninth century. It seems that one day Kaldi noticed that his flock became energized when eating certain berries, so he acted sheepishly, if not capriciously, and followed the example of his flock. After he got the same buzz, he related his discovery to some fellow Arab goatherds. Before long, other Arabs learned how to dry and boil the fruit. The brew became known as *qahwah* in Arabic and later in Turkish as *kahveh*. Some etymologists believe that the Arabic word derives from the name Kaffa, a city in the south Abyssinian highlands where the plant appears to be native. According to Arab lexicographers the *qahwah* originally referred to wine, or at least some kind of wine, and was a derivative of a verb root *qahiya*, "to have no appetite." Certainly today when one sees people drinking cup after cup, one might assume that they had no appetite for more substantial fare.

Around 1570, coffee made its European debut in Venice and by the end of the sixteenth century Italian traders introduced the beverage to other parts of Europe. It is said that some Christian zealots regarded the beverage to be a concoction of Satan and therefore asked Pontiff Clement VIII to forbid the faithful from imbibing it. Before giving judgement, His Holiness asked for a cup and then quickly decided that the beverage was so delicious that it would be sinful to have the pleasure of drinking it restricted to infidels.

ZERO

"Zero" ultimately descends from the Arabic *çifr*, from which we also get the word "cipher." Its first citation to denote the number 0 in English occurs in Edward Grimstone's 1604 translation of José de Acosta's widely cited *Historia natural y moral de las Indias* where he states: "They accompted their weekes by thirteeene dayes, marking the dayes with a Zero or cipher." As mathematicians remind us, the invention of nothing (or zero) was one of the more important discoveries in all mathematical history.

SHERBET

"Sherbet" joined our lexicon in 1603 and comes from a Turkish and Persian word of the same spelling which itself comes from the Arabic *shariba*, "to drink." The first *OED* definition of "sherbet" is "a cooling drink of the East, made of fruit juice and water, sweetened, often cooled with snow." This is borne out in its first citation in 1603 from Richard Knolles' *History of the Turkes*: "The guests dranke water prepared with sugar, which kind of drink they call Zerbet."

SERENDIPITY

On January 28, 1754, Horace Walpole wrote in a letter to his friend Horace Mann: "I once read a silly fairy tale called *The Three Princes of Serendip* [a former Arabic name for what is now known as Sri Lanka] . . . who were always making discoveries, by accidents . . . of things which they were not in quest of." He dubbed this faculty of making happy and unexpected discoveries "serendipity." Although created in the eighteenth century, there are few documented uses of the word until the twentieth century, when it became a favourite of university students of English.

TARIFF

If you hate all forms of taxation and are looking for a group to blame for the word "tariff," it should not be the residents of Tarifa, a small town on the southernmost coast of the Iberian Peninsula. Etymologically, however, you should point your finger at Arabs, since a *tarrif* in Arabic means "notification" or "definition." Its first English sense in the late sixteenth century is as an arithmetical table or statement. This was followed almost immediately by the modern sense of a list or schedule for the imposition of custom duties, or any item of the list, so that we speak of the tariff or tax on such things as cars.

TEN WORDS
You Never Knew Came
from Persian

As Persia (nowadays called Iran), in its glory days, possessed mighty armies that travelled far from home in their conquests, it is not surprising that many words of Persian lineage have filtered over the millennia into English. In *A History of Civilization*, Fernand Braudel relates that between the eighth and tenth centuries AD, "Persian made its presence felt subtly . . . as a language of scholarship and sophistication." By the sixteenth century many words of Persian lineage had permeated into English and the use of these words was reinforced by the British presence in India. Loanwords into English from Persian are similar to those from Arabic in that they are dominated by words that reflect luxury, materials and colour.

DIVAN

This word started out in Persian as *dēvān* and it originally meant a small book. Then it transformed to a book of accounts. From this sense, it extended its meaning to refer to official rooms such as a court or a council chamber. It then took on the restricted sense of part of a room, i.e. a long seat placed against the wall in luxurious chambers. Today, if it is used at all, it is likely to mean a couch or a couch that can also double as a bed. In *The Moon and Sixpence*, Somerset Maugham has a character comment, "I had a divan in my sitting room, and could very well sleep on that."

CANDY

It is said that the legions of Alexander the Great were introduced to a Persian delicacy which was composed of a reed garnished with spices, honey and colouring. This Persian treat was called *kand*, "juice of sugar cane," and this word derived from the old Arabic word for sugar, *quand*. Ultimately, candy comes from the Sanskrit *khanda* "piece of something," or "sugar in crystalline pieces."

The term "eye-candy," often used for a man or woman who is exceptionally attractive but lacking in all else, has recently become the newest use of the word. One might be tempted to apply the term to Alexander's great friend, Hephaestion, but this would be an error, for he also happened to be a great warrior.

LOZENGE

Some etymologists believe that this word derives ultimately from the Persian *lawz*, "almond," because of a similarity in shape between the two objects. It is first recorded in English in the fourteenth century with the meaning of "diamond-shaped." Its present sense of a medicated tablet comes about because, in the sixteenth century, the word was used to refer to small cakes of medicated or flavoured sugar that originally were diamond-shaped.

TULIP

Both words "tulip" and "turban" descend from the Persian *dulband*. The word was applied to the flower because of the flower's supposed resemblance to a turban. The first English "tulip" citing occurs in 1578 in Henry Lyte's *Herball*, which was itself a reworking of a book by Flemish physician Rembert Dodoens. The flower was introduced into Western Europe in the early seventeenth century by Dutch botanist Carolus Clusius. For Canadians, the tulip holds a special place in their national consciousness, since shortly after World War II, the Dutch people gave Ottawa some 100,000 tulip bulbs to say thanks for Canada's role in freeing Holland and offering the Dutch Royal family a safe place to live during the Nazi invasion.

PARADISE

John Milton may have given us *Paradise Lost*, but the ancient Persians provided paradise in the first place. *Paridaiz*, or "around built," referred to an enclosed park, orchard or pleasure ground. In Arabic, it was rendered as *pairidïaza* and it referred to a walled enclosure for virtuous Moslems after they died. This after-death sense was adopted into Old English by the ninth century, with the Garden of Eden representing an earthly paradise.

SPINACH

Popeye's favourite energy food goes back ultimately to the Persian, *aspanākh*, which became Arabic *isfināj*, then Latin *spinachia*. It has been postulated that the Latin word was adopted because of the spiny seeds found in some types of spinach.

MUSK

Musk is defined by the *OED* as "A reddish brown substance with a strong, persistent odour secreted by a gland of the male musk deer." The gland from which the deer secretes the musk was considered by the Persians to resemble a scrotum, so they adapted the Sanskrit word for scrotum, *muska*, into their word for musk, *mushk*. Today "musk" is likely to be applied to a sensual or sexual odour, but not necessarily linked to the male of the species.

❧ SCARLET

Most probably, this word comes from the Persian *saqalāt*, "rich cloth." This cloth could be many colours but, perhaps, since red represents one of the most common colours, by the fourteenth century "scarlet" took on a reddish hue. It is curious that the term is most often applied to the colour of a soldier's uniform or that of a high church dignitary but that it is also the colour of shame, as has been the case with not just a few Canadian churchmen of recent times.

❧ CHECKMATE/CHESS

The game of chess was developed in Persia in the sixth century, and if a player had his opponent's king trapped he announced *shāh-mat*, "the king is dead," i.e., "checkmate." While English derived the word "chess" from the Old French *eschec* (from which the word "check" comes), ultimately the French word comes from the Persian *shāh*, "king." According to *The Secret Life of Words* by Henry Hitchens, "An explanation for the game being known to Europeans by the name of just one of its six types of piece is that early travellers to the Middle East brought back the most handsome figurines — finely carved kings — as mementos of their time there."

Incidentally, the chess piece "rook" comes from the Persian *rukh*, whose original sense, according to the *OED*, is "doubtful."

❧ PAJAMA

The first definition of this word in the *OED* gives its original meaning as "loose trousers, usually of silk or cotton, tied round the waist, and worn by both sexes in some Asian and Middle Eastern countries." This was how the word was used in India but ultimately the word is Persian, where *pā* meant "foot" or "leg" and *jāma* referred to "clothing" or "garment." Today, Westerners think of pajamas (or pyjamas) as night attire, but the pajama is still worn as an everyday article of clothing in northern India by villagers. You can choose to spell the word either "pajama" or "pyjama," the latter tending to be more American.

TEN WORDS
You Never Knew Came
from India

In 1783, during the early days of what was soon to be the Raj, Sir William Jones was appointed chief justice in India. Jones took it upon himself to learn Sanskrit in order to understand fully Hindu and Muslim laws. Four years later, he observed that Sanskrit bore a stronger affinity to Greek and Latin, "both in the roots of verbs and in the forms of grammar, than could possibly have been produced by accident [and] that no philosopher could examine them all three without believing them to have sprung from some common source, which, perhaps, no longer exists."

The western world's Sanskrit legacy is apparent in many kinship words. The Sanskrit word for "father" is *pitr*, very similar to the Greek and Latin *pater*; "mother" in Sanskrit is *matr*, almost identical to Latin *mater*. Sanskrit *bhratr* became Old English *brodor*, German, Swedish and Danish *broder* and modern English "brother." *Svasa* in Sanskrit bequeathed us the Old English *sweoster*, the German *Schwester* and the modern English "sister."

The English language has absorbed many words from Sanskrit and the more modern languages of India such as Hindi. The lineage of many of these words, such as "nirvana," "mantra," "guru," "karma," "yoga," "tikka," "samosa" and "curry" are obviously Indian, but there are many others whose Indian flavour is not as apparent. As an appetizer, I will tell you that "cushy" does not derive from "cushion," as you might think, but comes from the Hindi word for "pleasant," *khush*.

Here are ten other hidden Indian delights.

২৮ SHAMPOO

If you massage your scalp when you give yourself a "shampoo," you are performing the proper etymological activity. "Shampoo" comes from the Hindi word *campo*, the imperative of *cāmpnā*, "to press." The first sense recorded in the *OED* is "to subject a person (his limbs) to massage." The first citation, dating from 1762, reflects an activity less sedentary than the one we associate with hair salons: "Had I not seen several China merchants shampooed before me, I should not have been apprehensive of danger." Clearly, shampooing in this context had something to do with violent massage. In *Dombey and Son*, Dickens relates how Miss Pankey was "shampooed every morning" — meaning that she was massaged. The common sense of "shampoo" to refer to the washing of hair emerged in the mid-nineteenth century. In fact, Thomas Chandler Haliburton from Nova Scotia is credited with introducing the term to the language in this sense in 1838 in his *Clockmaker* essays.

২৮ JUGGERNAUT

The word "juggernaut" is now employed metaphorically to refer to "a crushing force," such as "juggernaut of history," but originally the "crush" was literal. In Hinduism, Jagganath is a title of the god Krishna. The *OED* states that in Orissa, "the idol of this deity at Puri [is] annually dragged in procession on an enormous car, under the wheels of which many devotees are said to have formerly thrown themselves to be crushed." Even today, officials take care to ensure that no one throws themselves under the wheels of the god. In the United Kingdom, a "juggernaut" also can refer to a large heavy vehicle.

SWASTIKA

Probably the most notorious word we have absorbed out of India is "swastika" from Sanskrit which, ironically, is a marriage of *sú*, "good," and *astí*, "being." This is a word for an ancient good-luck symbol, deriving from the Sanskrit *svastí*, "well-being, fortune, luck." The first definition in the *OED* is "a primitive symbol or ornament of the form of a cross with equal arms with a limb of the same length projecting at right angles from the end of each arm, all in the same direction and (usually) clockwise." In Canada, until the late 1930s, the symbol was thought of in connection with "peace" and was frequently found on buildings. In fact there were a number of early women's ice hockey teams called the Swastikas, the Edmonton Swastikas being one of five in Canada. The Nazi Party then adopted the symbol, although it reversed the direction of the arms. In German it was referred to as the *Haken kreuz*. It is the karma of Sanskrit to have provided us with both the sweetness of "candy" *(khanda)* and the bitterness of "swastika."

LILAC

From Sanskrit we get the little-used word "anil," the West Indian shrub that is the source of the indigo dye. In Sanskrit, *nila* means "dark blue." This passed into Persian as *nil*, from which the word *nilak*, "bluish" was derived. This word, in turn, was absorbed by Arabic as *lilak*, from whence we were bequeathed the "lilac" plant with its familiar colour.

THUG

Although "thug" sounds as if it blends the words "thick" and "ugly," the *OED* explains it does not, but its description of "thug" makes it resemble a ghoulish tax-deductible organization or an investment bank:

"Association of professional robbers and murderers in India who strangled their victims." The actual name of this fraternal order was P'hanisigars, "noose operators," and the British euphemistically bequeathed them the name Thuggees or Thugs, from the Sanskrit word *sthaga*, meaning "cheater," which dates back to at least the thirteenth century. These Thugs were said to be honouring the Hindu goddess of destruction, Kali, through their mayhem. They operated in groups, often joining caravans of travellers and then secretly murdering large numbers. Their preferred method was strangulation with a noose, a technique that was taken over by commandoes in the two world wars. The British eliminated the Thugs in the 1830s, when they hanged over 500 of them and sentenced close to 3,000 to life imprisonment. The word "thug" lives on with the sense of a low-life hoodlum, one inclined or hired to treat another roughly or brutally.

PARIAH

The term "pariah" has become generalized over time. Originally, a pariah was a member of a very extensive low caste, the Paraiyars, in southern India, whose members supplied most of the domestics in European service. The name derives from the Tamil *parai*, "large drum," because the duty of the Paraiyars was to beat the drum at certain religious festivals. The British, incorrectly believing that the Paraiyars represented the lowest caste, adopted the word "pariah" to refer to any social outcast. Today it can be, and often is, used to refer to certain states.

TANK

In the Marathi language of India, the word *tanken* designates a reservoir of water, which is why early Portuguese colonizers referred to such reservoirs as *tanques*. The first citation of "tank" in the *OED* goes back to 1616 and states, "In India, a pool or lake, or an artificial reservoir or cistern, used for purposes of irrigation, and as a storage-place for drinking-water." The term "tank," to refer to an armoured military vehicle with tracks running all around, was first used in December 1915, and this word was chosen not for any metaphorical connection to a large container of liquids but strictly as a coded secret word. Several days after the unveiling of this new weapon, the *Times* reported, "'Tanks' is what these new machines are generally called, and the name has the evident official advantage of being quite undescriptive." The etymological grapevine, however, suggests that it was so named because of its resemblance to a benzene tank. As a verb it can mean two contradictory things. One can tank — meaning that one can go *down*, as in a tank. Or, one can tank *up*, which means to fill up, as in tanking up a car.

ORANGE

We may not know whether there were chickens before eggs or vice versa, but we do know that "orange," the fruit, preceded "orange," the colour. It derives from the Sanskrit name for the fruit *narangah*, "orange tree," which became the Persian *narang*, and Arabic *naranj* in Spain. According to John Ayto in *Dictionary of Word Origins*, "the Spanish form *naranj* filtered up to France and became altered (through the influence of Orange, the name of a town in southeastern France which used to be a centre of the orange trade) to *orenge*, later orange — whence the English word."

BUNGALOW

In Hindustani, *bangla* means "belonging to Bengal," and in the seventeenth century the British called any lightly built house in India with a thatched roof a "bungalow." Over time, the term became generalized for any single-storey house. On Cape Breton Island, in Nova Scotia, Canada, the term "bungalow" is used to refer to a summer cottage.

JUNGLE

The word "jungle" goes back to the Sanskrit *jagala*, "dry ground," or "desert," and the Hindi and Marathi *jangal*, "area of wasteland" — far different from our present sense of a moist, lush tropical forest. The *OED* states that "the change in Anglo-Indian use may be compared to that in the historical meaning of the word *forest* in its passage from a waste or unenclosed tract to one covered with wild wood. In the transferred sense of *jungle* there is apparently a tendency to associate it with *tangle*." By the middle of the nineteenth century "jungle" became metaphorical to refer to a tangled mess where presumably the "law of the jungle" prevailed. Indians still refer to any wild scrub land as a jungle, and the term can also be applied to Westerners who travel rough: "the junglee sahib."

FIFTY-FIVE WORDS
Whose Pedigree Will Delight
and Amuse You

≈

AFTERMATH

If you associate the word "aftermath" with "nuclear," take heart that the original sense was far less catastrophic. The "-math" segment is merely a variation of the word "mow" and "aftermath" originally referred to the second mowing of grass. The *OED* says that it is the "crop of grass which springs up after the mowing in early summer." This term arose in the fifteenth century, and within 150 years it came to refer to a usually unpleasant condition which results from some important event. Winston Churchill commented that "the life and strength of Britain . . . will be tested to the full, not in the war but in the aftermath of war." In fact, he himself was tested after the war since he was voted out of office — quite an aftermath!

ALBATROSS/ALCATRAZ

Ultimately, the name of the island prison Alcatraz can be traced back to the Arabic *al-quādūs*, which meant "the water bucket," used in the irrigation process. Alcatraz also gets its name because in Portuguese and Spanish *alcatraz* is the name for a pelican, which for aeons frequented the San Francisco bay area. The connection between birds and buckets arises from a mythical story among Portuguese sailors that the pelican — a bird they confused with the albatross — possessed a water pouch, so they nicknamed this bird *algatross*. It would seem that an etymologically-minded English mariner decided that since this bird was white, and *alba* is Latin for "white" that this bird should be called an albatross. The word "pelican" itself derives from the Greek *pelecus*, "hatchet," an allusion to the bird's beak.

AMOK

The first citation of "amok" in the *OED* dates from 1516, and offers the following quotation: "there are some of them (Javanese) who go into the streets, and kill as many as they meet. These are called Amuco." In some Southeast Asian cultures, men have been known to experience "amok," an episode of homicidal rage followed by forgetfulness. In any case, the word's first definition states that it is "a name for a frenzied Malay." According to *Marsden's Malay Dictionary*, *amoq* is defined as "engaging furiously in battle, attacking with desperate resolution, rushing in a state of frenzy to the commission of indiscriminate murder. . . . Applied to any animal in a state of vicious rage." I take issue with Marsden. The "commission of indiscriminate murder" is perpetrated only by one type of animal: *Homo sapiens*.

AMBITION

While nowadays we generally admire people with ambition, it was not always so. The first sense of the word in the *OED* is "The ardent (in early usage, inordinate) desire to rise to high position, or to attain rank, influence, distinction or other preferment." In 1593, in *Christ's Teares over Jerusalem*, Thomas Nashe penned, "Ambition is any puff up greedy humour of honour or preferment." It took on a positive hue only in the seventeenth century. Even today, however, one has to be careful with the word, for to be ambitious can easily topple into being overly ambitious.

✑ APRON

Like "umpire" that was originally rendered as "numpire" and the snakish "adder" that evolved from "nadder," the word "apron" derives from the Old French *naperon*. Hence, it is not surprising that the apron is connected to the word "napkin." Its affiliation with "map," however, is not so apparent. In Latin, *mappa* meant "napkin," "tablecloth" or "towel." When this word arrived in modern French, the "m" was changed into an "n" and this created the words *nappe*, "tablecloth," and *napperon*, "placemat." The "map" connection arose because in medieval Latin, representations of the world's surface were called *mappa mundi*, "tablecloth of the world" probably because their shape suggested a spread-out tablecloth. By the early sixteenth century, the word "map" was used in English to refer to a cartographic chart.

✑ ARSENIC

While arsenic might be a poison, etymologically it is a colour and ultimately derives from the Persian *zar*, "gold," and the Sanskrit *hari*, "yellowish." This is why the term "arsenic" was originally applied to the lemon-yellow mineral arsenic trisulphide. The word was borrowed into Arabic as *zernikh* and, as happens so often with Arab words, its definite article *al*, or "the," was perceived by foreigners as part of the word; hence *azzernikh* literally means "the arsenic trisulphide." This term was then borrowed into Greek as *arrenikon* and *arsenikon*. The Greek word *arren*, "male/virile," already existed and there was a belief that *arrenikon* could boost a male's potency, provided it was ingested in a non-lethal dose. The original English application of the word was to arsenic trisulphide and it is not until the early seventeenth century that the term is employed to describe its now common usage of white arsenic that is chemically the trioxide of arsenic.

𝒶 BALLOT

The word "ballot" derives from the Italian *ballotta*, "little ball." In days of yore, before the likes of voters in Florida in the 2000 American Presidential election were addled with pregnant, hanging or dimpled chads, people often voted by dropping little balls into a receptacle. The first *OED* citation in 1561 states: "Boxes into whiche if he wyll, he may let fall his ballot, that no man can perceiue hym." Related to "ballot" is the idea that since a white ball often meant a "yes" vote and a black ball designated a "no" vote, the term "blackball" came to refer to undesirability in the late eighteenth century. University frosh who have to undergo blackballing as a form of initiation also find it undesirable.

𝒶 BANKRUPT

"Bankrupt" comes from the Italian *bancarotta* which means "bank broken" or "bench broken," and this word recalls the provision that insolvent Venetian money-lenders destroy the tables they used while plying their trade. Samuel Johnson commented, "It is said that when an Italian money-changer became insolvent his 'bench was broke.'" In the sixteenth century the word "bankrupt" was often rendered as "banke rota." In fact, the word's first *OED* citation comes from *State Papers, Henry VIII*, in 1539 and states: "With danger to make with banke rota." In medieval times, and possibly even thousands of years earlier, money-lenders would transact their business on a small bench. The term "bankruptcy" came into vogue at the beginning of the eighteenth century but not before the terms "bankrupting," "bankruptism," "bankrupture," "bankruptship" had been employed for several decades. Interestingly, the term was already been used in a metaphorical sense in the seventeenth century, when Lyly, in his play *Euphues*, commented on those who are "Not onely unthrifts of their money but banckerouts of good manners."

BLURB

This word was coined as a hoax. The year was 1907 and the Retail Booksellers Association was hosting a dinner for American humourist and illustrator Gellett Burgess's new book *Are You a Bromide?* The descriptions on the book jackets of the day were even more flowery than those nowadays and Gellett decided to have some fun tampering with this tendency to extravagance. For the jacket of the book, Gellett fashioned a babelicious airhead he dubbed Blinda Blurb who, he claimed, was "blurbing a blurb to end all blurbs." Surprisingly, the word stuck and the *OED* first shows a citation for the word in 1914.

BOONDOCKS

Bundok is the word for "mountain" in Tagalog, the main language in the Philippines. During World War II, American soldiers extended the meaning to refer to any terrain that proved difficult to traverse. When the word was brought back to the United States, it at first referred to treacherous terrain on the periphery of training camps. Eventually the sense was extended to refer to non-desirable rural places, i.e., "the sticks" or "the boonies." I recall a '60s song entitled "Down in the Boondocks," whose lyrics included "Down in the boondocks, people put me down 'cause that's the side of town I was born in."

BOSS

The early American colonists disliked the term "master" because of its elitist allusions and were happy to import a more homey word from the Dutch. The Dutch word *baas* was originally rendered in English as "bass" or "base," and by the beginning of the nineteenth century "boss" became the definitive spelling. It is first recorded in the *OED* in 1649 but was considered too slangy for many a purist's tastes, some of whom were the upstart Americans. Nineteenth-century novelist James Fenimore Cooper, for one, declared "boss" to be a vulgarization of the English language. I do not, however, recommend anyone telling the boss that he/she is a "vulgarization" or "vulgarian."

I remember in the 1960s "boss" being used as a teenage slang synonym for "classy," but in fact its use in this sense far precedes my adolescent era. In nineteenth-century America, particularly in colloquial English, "boss" was often used to denote excellence. Mark Twain uses it in this manner in the following passage in *The Adventures of Huckleberry Finn*: "It's the most dazzling idea 'at ever a man struck. You have cert'nly got the most astonishin' head I ever see. Oh, this is the boss dodge, ther' ain't no mistake 'bout it."

CAUCUS

This word is generally believed to have an Amerindian origin. Both in form and meaning, it is almost identical to the word *caucauasu* which means "counsellor" in the Algonquin languages. In 1624, Captain John Smith of Pocahontas lore reported in his *Generall Historie of Virginia* that "the Indians are governed by the Priests and their Assistants, or their Elders called *Caw-cawwas-soughes*." In the eighteenth century when political leaders in Boston met to select candidates for elections they dubbed their meeting "a caucus." In the late nineteenth century this term caught on in England and other parts of the English-speaking world. In Canadian circles, one also refers to the caucus of political parties, such as the Liberal caucus or the NDP caucus, meaning the members of the legislature of that party.

CHAGRIN

This word's first *OED* definition is "A species of skin or leather with a rough surface." It came into English through French but ultimately can be traced back to the Turkish *saghri* that referred to the rump of a horse, a rather rough and leathery surface. In any case, probably due to the texture of a horse's posterior, it also was the word used for roughened leather. The word *chagrin* first appeared in French in the fourteenth century with the sense of "sad, vexed," and I suppose a material that rubbed you the wrong way would leave you in this state. In English, in the seventeenth century, it referred to anxiety or melancholy but in the eighteenth century, according to the *OED*, it took on the specific sense of "Acute vexation, annoyance, or mortification, arising from disappointment, thwarting, or failure." One can imagine that it was with some chagrin that Stephen Harper visited the Governor General to prorogue parliament. From the looks of things, on the second occasion, he acted not with chagrin, but alacrity, for a telephone call sufficed.

CHOCOLATE

The Aztecs drank a blend of cacao dissolved in water to which they sometimes added corn and sapodilla kernels; they called this concoction *xocolatl*, or *chocolatl*, and believed that this drink possessed not only nutritional value but aphrodisiac qualities as well. The *OED*'s first definition of chocolate is "an article of food made of equal parts of the seeds of cacao and those of the tree called *pochotl*." This word was a compound formed from *xococ*, "bitter," and *atl*, "water." Now in a game of Password, the clue "chocolate" is much more likely to elicit the answer "sweet" rather than "bitter" or "water." This is because noted conquistador and ethnic cleanser Hernando Cortes, who had been introduced to chocolate by Aztec Emperor Montezuma, reasoned that if this bitter beverage was blended with sugar it could become a commercial hit in the Old Country. Possibly because of chocolate's purported effect on the libido, the Vatican felt it necessary to meet in 1569 to decide on this sensual concoction and decided that it was still permissible to eat chocolate on Fridays. In the early part of the seventeenth century confectioners developed a crude type of chocolate bar, consisting of the chocolate paste, sugar and spices. The product was a very coarse one at best, and because of the high price of cocoa beans, probably contained more spice than chocolate.

In the early nineteenth century Dutchman Conrad van Houten developed and patented a process for extracting the fat from the cocoa beans to create powdered cocoa and cocoa butter. Van Houten discovered that by treating chocolate with an alkalizing agent it helped neutralize the bitter taste. Today many of the chocolate bars on sale in the stores contain very little chocolate, and a true chocolate lover may reject the chocolate bar altogether as mere candy.

CHOP SUEY

Jennifer 8. Lee, in her book *The Fortune Cookie Chronicles*, describes this word as the "greatest culinary prank one culture has ever played on another" because this food, once thought by many Americans to be the national dish of China, merely means "mixed bits" in Cantonese. It is still one of the mainstays of many Canadian-Chinese restaurants found in small towns.

COACH

The word "coach" (as in "carriage") derives from the town of Kocs in northwestern Hungary. In the fifteenth century an unknown carriage maker in Kocs developed a larger, more comfortable carriage than any known at the time. It was called a *Koczi szeter*, "wagon of Kocs," which was shortened to *kocsi*. It was rendered as *coche* in Portuguese, French and English. By the sixteenth century it was being spelled in English as "coach." The other sense of coach, "trainer," came about as university slang in the nineteenth century. The notion here is of a tutored student being transported through an examination as if he were riding in a coach.

COOKIE

"Cookie" doesn't come from "cook" but from "cake," as it derives from the Dutch *koekje*, diminutive of *koek*. It was brought to America by

Dutch settlers of New Amsterdam, later called New York, and served as a Dutch treat on New Year's Day. According to David Barnhart and Allan Metcalf in *America in So Many Words*, "During the 1700s the sweet, flat little cakes became the favorites of all New Yorkers of all backgrounds." In 1786, on perhaps a slow news day, a New York newspaper wrote an editorial bemoaning "idle boys, who infest our ... streets, with baskets of cookies." Maybe that's where Sesame Street got the idea for the Cookie Monster? Here's a test for your memory: what is his favourite kind of cookie?

CUSHY

This word has hardly changed from its Hindi origin *khush* or Urdu *kusht* that meant "pleasant" or "excellent." The word "cushy" originated in Anglo-Indian slang in the early twentieth century. It most likely became popular because of the association of a cushion being both pleasant and comfortable. The first *OED* citation of "cushy" is in 1915 and the word bears no etymological connection to "cushion," which came from the Old French *coisson*.

DOILY

'Tis said that in the latter part of the seventeenth century, a certain Mr. Doiley or Doyley owned a famous drapers shop on the Strand in London. An article by Eustache Budgell in *The Spectator* on January 24, 1712, states, "The famous Doily is still fresh in every one's Memory, who raised a Fortune by finding out Materials for such Stuffs as might at once be cheap and genteel." The name "doily" was first applied to a light fabric used for summer wear and then to a variety of ornamental table napkins. In the nineteenth century the word came to be used for a decorative lacy mat usually made of paper or linen that is put on plates

[ANSWER: chocolate chip]

under party food to add panache. Disposable paper doilies are still in use — hardly the "genteel" item that Mr. Spectator mentioned in 1712.

🌿 DOLLAR

Surprisingly, the almighty dollar originated in the Bohemian silver mining town of Sankt Joachimsthal in the early part of the sixteenth century. A silver coin minted here was called a *Joachimsthaler*, and this was shortened to *thaler*. In the 1550s this word arrived in England as "dollar," and the term designated not only German coins but also the Spanish peso. In the United States the dollar was established as the official monetary unit in 1785, while in Canada the term was adopted in 1858. In fact, there was much wrangling over many years about whether to continue with the British sterling system or the American decimal system, and for a time in different parts of the country both were used. As with so many things, the American system finally prevailed, although Newfoundland based its system on the Spanish dollar.

🌿 ENGINEER

One thinks of an engineer as a person who constructs useful things such as pontoons and aqueducts, but in the thirteenth century the primary sense of "engineer" was of a person who laid snares or hatched nasty political plots. Even as late as 1594, Gabriel Harvey, in *Pierces Supererogation, or a new prayse of the old asse*, writes of "The dreadfull enginer of phrases insteede of thunderboltes." Later, the word was first applied to constructors of military engines and eventually to someone who constructs any object of public utility.

🌿 FACT

The word "fact" appears often in Shakespeare's plays and in all cases it refers to a wicked deed or a crime. In *Macbeth*, the nobleman Lennox, referring to the manner of Duncan's death, says to one of the Lords,

"Damned fact, / How it did grieve Macbeth," and in *1 Henry VI*, Glou-
cester, referring to Falstaff's cowardliness, states that "this fact was infa-
mous." The *OED* notes that the first senses of the word in the 1540s were
"a thing done or performed" or "a noble or brave deed" but adds that in
the sixteenth and seventeenth centuries the most common sense was of
"an evil deed, a crime." It adds that this sense lives on in expressions such
as "confess the fact" and "after the fact" or "before the fact." The *OED*
provides citations for the miscreant sense of "fact" until the second half
of the nineteenth century. Perhaps this is what Jack Webb's character of
a police sergeant had in mind on the 1950s television drama *Dragnet*
when he would plead with female witnesses "Just the facts, ma'am." In
our own postmodern world, the very notion of "fact" as fact, or something undeniably true, seems to be under erasure.

FASCIST

Not too many people will be overwhelmed to discover that "fascist"
comes from Italian. However, its Latin etymology is quite interesting.
The word ultimately derives from the Latin *fascis*, which referred to a
bundle of sticks. In ancient Rome this bundle coupled with a protrud-
ing axe was the symbol of official power. The axe blade represented the
punishing force of the state and the removal of the axe from the *fascis*
declared the sovereignty of the citizens of Rome. Because a bundle of
sticks is tightly-knit, *fascis* came to refer to a cohesive political unit, and
in 1919 Benito Mussolini formed a political party that he dubbed *Fasci
italiani di combattimento*. Although the term "fascist" nowadays bears
more than a soupçon of negativity, it was not always the case. In 1921,
the *Literary Digest* carried an essay that averred, "Not all the doings of
the Fascisti can be commended, nor is Fascism free from disquieting
symptoms; but without its daring energy Italy would probably have felt
the grip of Asiatic Jacobinism and have gone through a period of terrible
dissolution." Yes, getting the railways to run on time has always been a
plus for the Fascists.

FIASCO

In Italian, *fiasco* means "flask" or "bottle." The *OED* states that "the figurative use of the phrase *far fiasco* (literally 'to make a bottle') in the sense 'to break down or fail in a performance' is of obscure origin," and many etymological theories abound. One guess is that when an early Venetian glassblower discovered a flaw developing in a beautiful piece he was working on, he transformed it into an ordinary bottle rather than destroying it. This plain bottle would then represent failed art to the glassblower. Another theory indicates that the word derives from the Italian *fare il fiasco*, which once referred to playing a game in which the loser pays for "the fiasco," i.e. "the bottle of wine." Still another hypothesis claims that the flask in question was a powder flask, and the original fiasco occurred in battle when the powder burnt or exploded while still in the flask, thus sidelining the unfortunate musketeer.

Complicating matters even further, the *OED* states that "alleged incidents in Italian theatrical history are related to account" for the origin of "fiasco" but does not pass on any of these fanciful theatrical tales. A footnote in the 1846 American journal *Littel's Living Age* states, "Few of our readers can be unfamiliar with the meaning of *Fiasco*, a cant word used throughout Italy to designate a failure, especially in theatrical matters." Even among Italian etymologists there is no consensus about the word, so for the moment, the true origin of "fiasco" is truly a fiasco.

FILIBUSTER

The word "filibuster" ultimately comes from the Dutch *vrijbuiter*, "freebooter." The *OED* defines "freebooter" as "one who goes in search of plunder, especially a pirate." Between 1850 and 1860 the term referred specifically to bands of adventurers who organized expeditions from the United States, with the intent of revolutionizing certain countries in Central America and the Spanish West Indies. By the end of the nineteenth century, the term gained its political dimension of long-winded rhetoric to hold up legislation, the notion of piracy being attached to the political technique that holds a piece of legislation captive. Interestingly, although the original Dutch term was *vrijbuiter*, both French and Spanish absorbed the word into their language in a similar fashion to English: French as *filibustier* and Spanish as *filibustero*.

GAMBIT

The *OED* states that a "gambit" is "a method of opening the game, in which with the sacrifice of a pawn or piece the player seeks to obtain some advantage over his opponent." It says that the word comes from the Italian *gambetto*, "tripping up the heels" (in the context of wrestling). *Gambetto* itself derives from *gamba*, "leg," and it was borrowed into Spanish as *gambito* where the notion of an "underhanded procedure" was first applied to a chess manoeuvre in 1561 in Spanish, and in English in 1656. Now of course "gambit" is used in a much wider, more figurative sense. For example, one might say that the politician's assertion that there will be an increase of 5 percent in income tax is an opening gambit to make people accept the intended increase of "only" three percent.

GERRYMANDER

American politician Elbridge Gerry's redrawing of the map of the voting districts of Massachusetts in the late eighteenth century was said to resemble a salamander. "Gerry" was joined to the last two syllables of "salamander" to produce "gerrymander," which is defined as "to divide a state, county or city into voting districts to give unfair advantage to one party in elections." Gerry's scheming nature obviously stood him in good stead, for he went on to serve as vice-president of the United States from 1813–14 in the administration of James Madison.

GUNG HO

Ironically, this unofficial motto of the US Marine Corps is an expression of the Chinese Communist work ethic. Thus, it's surprising that the word was not investigated by Senator Joseph McCarthy in the 1950s. The word derives from the Mandarin *kung ho*, "work together." It was adopted into English in World War II by Evans Carlson, a US Marine colonel, during his commission in China. Carlson greatly admired the fighting spirit of his Red Chinese foes and he organized *kung-hoi* meetings in order to promote greater cooperation among his troops. The original sense of enthusiasm has been somewhat superseded by a sense of overzealousness.

HEARSE

The word "hearse" comes from the Latin *hirpex*, which sounds as if it refers to a virulent virus but actually was a harrow that was dragged over plowed land to break up clumps of earth. "Hearse" was also used to refer to an elaborate framework used for handing candles and other items over a coffin during a church service. Shakespeare uses the word in *Julius Caesar* to refer to a coffin, and fifty years later it came to refer to the carriage constructed for transporting the coffin. Literally, "rehearse" means to "harrow once more" and metaphorically first took on the sense of "repeat," then "repeat aloud" and "finally practice for a performance."

HORDE

The *OED*'s first definition of "horde" is "A tribe or troop of Tartar or kindred Asiatic nomads, dwelling in tents or wagons, and migrating from place to place for pasturage, or for war or plunder." It adds that the Golden Horde was the name for a tribe who possessed the khanate of Kiptchak, in Eastern Russia and western and central Asia, from 1400 to 1480. Ultimately, the word goes back to the Turkish *ordū*, "camp," that was rendered in Russian as *ordá* and in Polish as *horda*. It is also the source of the word "Urdu," as in the Urdu language of Pakistan and northern India. Etymologically, "Urdu" means "language of the camp." By the seventeenth century, "horde" had acquired the sense of a large number of people, more often than not behaving in an uncivilized manner.

HOT DOG

Lore has it that in 1900, sports cartoonist Thomas Aloysius "Tad" Dorgan was ingesting a sausage at the New York Polo Grounds, the baseball Giants' home park. Since there had been rumours that canine meat was being put into the sausages, he dubbed his bunned lunch "hot dog." His subsequent caricature of a dachshund on a bun got the goat of the Coney Island Chamber of Commerce who instituted a policy of banning the term "hot dog" by concessionaires, insisting instead on the use of PC terms such as "Coney Islands," "red hots" or "frankfurters." The Dorgan etymology has been repeated by many language writers including Bill Bryson in his book *Made in America*.

There are, however, some problems with this account. Dorgan was working in San Francisco in 1900 and did not move to New York until 1903. Also, no one has uncovered the Dorgan cartoon in question. He did, however, sketch some "hot dog" cartoons in 1906 from a bicycle race in Madison Square Gardens.

The first known use of the term "hot dog" is in the *Yale Record* in 1895; apparently the word "dog" had been a university slang term for "sausage" for at least a decade. But decades before, there had been accusations that sausage-makers were "dogging" their product. An article in the *New York Commercial Advertiser* of July 6, 1838, quipped, "Sausages have fallen in price one half in New York since the dog killers have commenced operations."

HYPOCRITE

This word in Greek merely meant "actor on a stage," but when it was adopted into English in the thirteenth century it referred to a person who pretends to have feelings or beliefs of a higher order than his real ones. Given that the present Governor of California, Arnold Schwarzenegger, was an actor along with a previous one (Ronald Reagan), is it fair to say that Californians like to elect hypocrites to govern their state? Perhaps not, since Schwarzenegger, unlike Reagan, is bringing in quite progressive legislation to slow down climate change.

JAZZ

Although the field of etymology endeavours to ascribe definitive origins to all words, you may have noticed by now that the reality is far more elusive, and the origins of many words are shrouded in legend. At times, we're not even sure of the identity of the bedfellow(s). Such is the murky situation of the origin of "jazz."

One theory states that the word derives from a slave by the name of Jasper who lived in a plantation near New Orleans in 1825. Another hypothesis claims that the progenitor of the word is Jasbo Brown, an itinerant black musician who played in Mississippi River towns and later in Chicago cabarets at the turn of the twentieth century. An etymology that has gained widespread currency among musicians credits Chaz Washington, a ragtime drummer from Vicksburg, Mississippi, circa 1904, as the word's founder. Geneva Smitherman, professor of English at Michigan State University, speculates that the term may ultimately come out of Africa from the Mandingo word *jasi*, "to act out of the ordinary."

Still another theory holds that the word comes from the French verb *jaser* that means "to chatter." This may not be such a far-fetched idea. After all, French was spoken in New Orleans either in the form of Creole or the Acadien of the early settlers transported from Nova Scotia and New Brunswick.

Actually, etymologists can't say with any certainty whether the French term *jaser* preceded the English term "jazz" or vice-versa. In the early nineteenth century when French-speaking white slave-owners fled from Haiti with their slaves to New Orleans, Louisiana was a French possession. Black slaves were also imported to Louisiana directly from

Africa; some were supplied by French slave traders and others by English slave traders. African slaves did not tend to preserve their original languages as they were mixed with people who spoke African languages that they did not understand. As a result, they developed pidgin languages in which much of their vocabulary was adopted from the language of their masters.

✑ KETCHUP

The Chinese invented *ke-tsiap* — a concoction of pickled fish and spices (but hold the tomatoes) — in the 1690s. By the early part of the eighteenth century its popularity had spread to Malaysia, where British explorers first encountered it. By 1740 the sauce, renamed "ketchup," was an English staple, and it was becoming popular in the American colonies. Tomato ketchup wasn't invented until the 1790s, when New England colonists first mixed tomatoes into the sauce. The reason that it took so long to add tomatoes to the sauce was that for most of the eighteenth century people had assumed they were poisonous, for the tomato is a close relative of the toxic belladonna and nightshade plants.

✑ KIOSK

We think of a kiosk as simply a place that sells newspapers but its origin is more exotic. The first definition in the *OED* describes it as "an open pavilion or summerhouse of light construction, often supported by pillars and surrounded with a balustrade; common in Turkey and Persia." It derives from the Turkish *kiūshk*, "pavilion," and the Persian *kūskh*, "palace, portico." In Britain, "telephone kiosks" used to be everywhere, but now with the cellular phone, they are fast disappearing.

✑ KOWTOW

The word "kowtow" in English bears the taint of obsequiousness, but its origin in Chinese doesn't connote an act of servility. It comes from the words *k'o*, "knock," and *t'ou*, "the head," and derives from the Chinese custom of touching the ground with the forehead as an expression of extreme respect. Its first use as a verb occurred in Benjamin Disraeli's 1827 novel *Vivian Grey*, and here already it is used in a figurative sense: "The Marquess kotooed like a first-rate Mandarin . . . ."

⤳ LOO

The British colloquial word "loo," for "toilet," was established by the 1920s. Its first citation in the *OED* is from James Joyces's *Ulysses* in 1922, is punnish, and does not offer any clue as to its derivation: "O yes, *mon loup*. How much cost? Waterloo. Watercloset."

Here is a synopsis of the major theories as to the origin of "loo":

- It derives from the word "ablutions" which was used by the British military in World War I to refer to a building on a base (sometimes called an "ablution hut") that contained wash-places and lavatories.

- Its progenitor was Père Bourdaloue, a celebrated seventeenth-century French preacher whose sermons were so long that it was said that it was advisable to carry a chamber pot (which came to be known as a *bourdalou*) if one intended to listen to an entire homily.

- It derives from the seventeenth-century Scottish term *gardyloo* uttered as a warning to people on ground level that a chamber pot was about to be emptied out of an upper-storey window.

- It comes from the French *l'eau*.

- It is an alternative spelling of *lew* which is a form of "lee" (shelter); in this case the word is euphemistic in nature, just as the sea unfortunately is sometimes used as a substitute toilet.

- It derives in some manner from the French word *lieu*, "place," which could be a shortened form of *lieu d'aisance*, literally "place of easement," a term that was encountered by British servicemen in World War I in France.

- It comes from the term *looard*, a dialectical form of "leeward," referring to the leeward part of a small boat being used as a toilet in the absence of other facilities.

- It is a clipping of "Waterloo," as in the battle of.

- It is a misreading of room number 100, supposedly a common European toilet location, for the word "loo" looks as though it could be the number 100.

Seeing that the word "loo" is first recorded in 1922, I find it unlikely that the term derived prior to the twentieth century. In itself, the date would rule out many of the theories, including "looard," "lew," "bourdalou" and "gardyloo," as being the source of "loo." In the case of "bourdalou," this term was rarely used in French vocabulary by the beginning of the twentieth century. With reference to "gardyloo": while Scotland had much closer ties with France than England did, and there are other examples where mangled French made its way into Scottish street language (e.g., *dinnae fash yerself* from *ne vous fachez pas*), it is unlikely that the term would remain dormant for over 300 years before emerging as "loo."

On the other hand, it is during World War I, when there was much language mixing, that the term was most likely absorbed into English. Interestingly, many European languages have slang terms for the toilet that approximate the sound of "loo." In German there is *klo*, short for *klosett*, and *lokus*, a term for a lavatory, while Dutch has the "loo" term *plee*. But it is the French word *lieu* which would be my leading candidate as the source of "loo." The euphemism "place of easement" was used to some extent in England and the euphemistic use of "place" for "toilet" is common in other languages such as Swedish *stalle* and *ett visst ställe*, and German *oertchen*. One can easily imagine how an English soldier would shorten *lieu d'aisance* to "loo," or that upon reading a French lavatory sign saying something like *On est prié de laisser ce lieu aussi propre qu'on le trouve*, the word *lieu* would resonate and then morph into "loo." I suppose once the term "loo" caught on, puns would proliferate, such as pronouncing "ablutions" as "ab-loo-tions" and referring to the toilet as the "waterloo." The "waterloo" pun would have been appreciated even by the French because *le water* (short for "water closet") has long been a French expression for "lavatory," and the term *le waterloo* may have represented an Anglo-Gallic pun. After "loo" was established, it would seem natural that a toilet facility marked room "100" would be rendered as "loo."

Of course, this is all conjectural because during those chaotic World War I years so many people learned smatterings of foreign languages that we will never know the definitive manner in which new slang terms, like "loo," came into English.

MATTRESS

In Arabic, *matrah* refers to a place where something is thrown, so we can only assume that early travellers to the Levant noticed the Arab penchant for sleeping on plush cushions scattered around a room. The word arrived in English in the fourteenth century via Italian *materasso* and Old French *materas*.

MORPHINE

This opiate's name derives from the god Morpheus. This god was created by the Roman poet Ovid when he was writing *Metamorphoses* around 5 AD. In the process of working on *Metamorphoses*, Ovid became interested in the realm of dreams, which he considered to exist in a dimension that transcended sleep. There already existed a god of sleep, the Greek god Somnus, which has bequeathed us the word "somnolent." So Ovid took the Greek word for "shape" and manufactured the god Morpheus that he described as the god of dreams that takes human shapes. Morphine is first cited in the *OED* in 1821 but the word came from French where it appeared four years earlier. Notwithstanding Ovid's dichotomy between sleep and dream, morphine is more guaranteed to make you sleep than dream.

NEPOTISM

This word comes from the Latin word for "nephew," *nepos*, and it refers to the showing of special favours to relatives in the conferring of some privilege or occupation. Apparently, some of the early (childless) popes conferred a preferred status or ecclesiastical opportunities on their nephews. It was also extended to their illegitimate sons. Today it means giving special favour not just to illegitimate children but to anyone within one's family or sphere of influence.

NERD/GEEK

The word "nerd" appears to have been derived from a fictional animal found in Theodore Geisel's (aka Dr. Seuss) story *If I Ran the Zoo*, written in 1950. This creature was depicted as a small, unkempt, humanoid creature with a large head and a comically disapproving expression. The following year *Newsweek* magazine stated, "In Detroit, someone who once would be called a drip or a square is now, regrettably, a nerd." The term, however, did not become popular until the late '60s when it became a shibboleth among college students and surfers to mark those considered "uncool." The cousin of "nerd" — "geek" — has its first *OED* citation in 1876 in a glossary of words from northern England where it is defined as "a fool; a person uncultivated; a dupe." It was also used in the United States for a good part of the twentieth century to refer to circus performers who performed bizarre feats such as biting off the head of a chicken. Robertson Davies uses it in this sense in his novel *Fifth Business*. Its first usage in the modern context occurs in a letter written in 1957 by writer Jack Kerouac and the word is used in a clearly depreciative manner. "Unbelievable number of events almost impossible to remember, including . . . Brooklyn College wanted me to lecture to eager students and big geek questions to answer." The word's origin is uncertain but it is generally believed to be a variation for the word "geck," a word that arose in the sixteenth century to refer to a simpleton.

Personally, I don't mind being called a nerd or a geek. In fact, I write a language column that I have titled "Word Nerd." Just don't call me a dweeb, doofus, or dork.

❧ OKAY/OK

"Okay" has been called by polemicist H.L. Mencken "the most shining and successful Americanism ever invented." Mencken reported that US troops deployed overseas during World War II found it already in use by Bedouins in the Sahara all the way to the Japanese in the Pacific. Since then it has spread to every corner of the world. As befits a ubiquitous term, it has had many false claimants as its source. Here are some of the pretenders:

- It comes from the Greek *ola kala*, "everything is well."

- It derives from the Scottish *och aye*, "okay."

- It is an English rendering of *aux quais*, "at the quays."

- It derives from Aux Cayes, a port on the southern coast of Haiti.

- It comes from the Choctaw term *okeh*, meaning "it is so."

- It derives from the West African language Ewe, where the word meant "good."

- It derives from the Indian chief Old Keokuk, who is said to have initialed treaties in the early nineteenth century.

- It stands for Obadiah Kelly, a railroad freight agent, or Orrin Kendall, a supplier of crackers to soldiers in the American Civil War.

- It derives from the German *ordnungsgemaess kontrolliert*, meaning "properly checked."

To understand the origin of "okay" we have to go back to the penchant for initialisms in America in the 1830s. Much like today where phrases on the Internet such as "in my opinion" and "on the other hand" become

"IMO" and "OTOH" respectively, in that era phrases such as "remains to be seen" and "small potatoes" might be rendered as "R.T.B.S" and "S.P." Some of these initialisms could be quite long such as "G.T.D.H.D.," "Give the Devil His Due." A New York newspaper in 1839 reported that a fashionable young lady remarked to her beau, "O.K.K.B.W.P." The young man paused momentarily then kissed her. The reporter decoded the initialism as "One Kind Kiss Before We Part." There was also the fashion of deliberate misspellings in humorous writing. Many American humorists from the 1820s on adopted as public personae uneducated country bumpkins who expressed their ideas in rural dialects rendered obtuse by deliberate misspellings. Hence "all right" was transformed to "O.W." on the basis of "oil wright"; "no use" was sometimes rendered as "K.Y.," "know yuse." In this context, it is believed that "OK" was fashioned after "oyl korrect" by Charles Gorden Greene, the editor of the *Boston Morning Post* on March 23, 1839. Greene referenced the editor of the *Salem Gazette* having the "contribution box . . . o.k — all correct — and cause the corks to fly, like *sparks*, upward." On April 12, the expression appeared in the *Salem Gazette* in the modern sense, "The house was O.K. at the last concert, and did credit to the musical taste of the ladies and gents."

Aside from "OK," living remnants of this craze for initials include "N.G." "no good" and "P.D.Q." or "pretty damn quick." Most of the other initialisms such as "O.F.M." ("our first men") died out, and this may have been the fate of "OK" except for the presidential election of 1840. In that year, the Democrats in New York created an O.K. Club which was derived from Old Kinderhook, after Kinderhook, New York, the birthplace of Martin Van Buren, the Democratic candidate. The abbreviation became widely used during the campaign and survived Van Buren's losing the election to William Henry Harrison. What also boosted the popularity of "OK" was the tale propagated by Van Buren's opponents that "OK" originated in 1828 by orthographically challenged Democratic presidential candidate Andrew Jackson. They said "OK" represented "ole korrek," Jackson's feeble attempt to spell "all correct." (Jackson may have indeed used "ole korrek" on a document, but he was just as liable to have spelled it four other ways on the same document.)

In any case by 1840, "OK" was firmly entrenched. Here are some other early citations: Sept 2, 1839, *Evening Tattler* (N.Y.), "These 'wise men from the East' . . . are right . . . to play at bowls with us as long as we are willing to set ourselves up, like skittles, to be knocked down for their amusement and emolument. OK! all correct!"; Oct. 11, 1839, *Boston Evening Transcript*, "Our Bank Directors have not thought it worth their while to call a meeting, even for consultation, on the subject. It is O.K. (all correct) in this quarter"; March 28, 1840, *Newark Daily Advertiser*, "The war cry of the locofocos was O.K., the two letters paraded at the head of an inflammatory article in the New Era of the morning. 'Down with the whigs, boys, O.K.' was the shout of these poor, deluded men"; Dec 15, 1840, *Boston Daily Times*, "What is't that ails the people, Joe? They're in a kurious way, for every where I chance to go, There's nothing but O.K."

Is it a word, a phrase, an abbreviation or an acronym? Whether you spell it "O.K.," "OK," "o.k." or "okay," whether it's rendered as a noun, verb, adjective or adverb, OK is okay.

OMBUDSMAN

The first definition of this word in the *OED* is "an official appointed by the Swedish parliament to investigate complaints against maladministration by central government and the civil service." The word in Swedish refers to a legal representative or adviser. Going back to Old Norse, however, we find the word *umbothsmathr*, "manager." In the 1960s, the word in English took on the specific sense of a person appointed by the government to investigate an individual's complaints about public authorities. Today there is a move to change to "ombudsperson."

PANOPLY

Originally, a "panoply," from the Greek *panaplia* (*pan*, "all" + *hopla*, "armour"), referred to a complete set of armour. At the end of the eighteenth century, however, the sense of the word became generalized and could refer to any complete covering or protective layer, even those of a spiritual nature.

ROBOT

In Karl Capek's 1920 play *R.U.R.*, mechanical men manufactured by the Rossum Universal Robot Corporation are designed to perform manual labour. However, they become uppity, revolt and eventually destroy mankind. The term robot comes from the Czech word *robotnik*, "slave," but ultimately derives from the Czech *robota*, which means "forced labour" and "work." Capek's play opened in both New York and London in 1923 and immediately the word passed into the English language. An issue of the *London Times* in 1923 stated, "If Almighty God had populated the world with Robots, legislation of this sort might have been reasonable." Within a couple of years the word was used to refer to people largely devoid of emotions. The U.S. Census Bureau defines a robot as a "multifunctionable manipulator designed to move material . . . or specialized devices through variable programmed motions for the performance of . . . tasks." Hmmm. Sounds eerily like a lot of jobs.

SEERSUCKER

According to the *OED*, this word came about as an "East Indian corruption of the Persian *shīr o shakkar*, literally, 'milk and sugar.'" Later on the sense transferred to a striped linen garment. One would assume that this is an allusion to the appearance of stripes, in the same manner that "salt and pepper" refers to a fine mixture of black and white. Fortunately no one refers to hair as being "seersucker" as one does with "salt and pepper," although with all the stripes showing up these days in tinted hair, perhaps the day is not far off. A new trend?

SMUGGLER/YACHT

The word "smuggler" itself comes from the Dutch *smokkelaar*, and the first *OED* citation from 1661 is more faithful to the Dutch spelling than the modern English rendition: "A sort of leud people called Smuckellors, rarely heard of before these late disordered times, who make it their trade . . . to steal and defraud His Majesty of His Customs." The Dutch are consequently responsible for another word related to these marauding folk. In the sixteenth century the Dutch began building light, speedy vessels designed to chase the ships of pirates and smugglers. These vessels were called *jaghtschips*, literally "ships for chasing," and the word "yacht" is first recorded in English in 1557.

SOFA

The word "sofa" ultimately comes from the Arabic *suffah*, which means "cushion or long bench." The first *OED* definition of this word states: "In Eastern countries, a part of the floor raised a foot or two, covered with rich carpets and cushions, and used for sitting upon," and the first citation in 1625 states: "A Sofa spread with very sumptuous Carpets of Gold . . . upon which the Grand Signior sitteth." "Chesterfield" is a Canadianism that emerged in the 1920s but the term has been declining in use since the 1970s. In a study done in Vancouver in 1984, *The Oxford Guide to Canadian English Usage* shows that while 72 percent of people used the term "chesterfield," only 30 percent used the term exclusively. "Sofa" and "couch" were the preferred terms. A survey done among Montreal anglophones in the late 1990s showed "sofa" and "couch" as being equally popular, with "chesterfield" being used by only 12 percent of respondents.

⌇ SOPHISTICATED

For those whose aim is sophistication, be aware that the *OED*'s first definition of the word declares you to be a sophomoric reprobate: "The use or employment of sophistry; the process of investing with specious fallacies or of misleading by means of these; falsification." Sophists, in case you weren't paying attention in your Philosophy 101 classes, were ancient Greek philosophers who, unlike the noble Socratic school of philosophy, didn't believe in truth for truth's sake, but rather trained pupils to get ahead in life. If you happen to be a trained student in your sophomore year, please do not take umbrage that etymologically speaking you are a "wise fool."

⌇ SUBSIDY

In the ancient Roman armies the *subsidii*, the plural of *subsidium*, referred to troops kept in reserve to provide support at critical battle junctures. In the late fourteenth century, the word "subsidie" was used in English to mean "aid." According to the *OED*, in the fifteenth century it was employed in England to refer to "pecuniary aid granted by parliament to the sovereign to meet special needs." In the nineteenth century, a "subsidy" came to refer to state assistance given to corporations or organizations.

⌇ TEA

Tea was born in the Yunnan province of China. It is claimed that the first tea seeds were brought to Japan by the returning Buddhist priest Yeisei, who had seen the value of tea in enhancing religious meditation in China. It would not be until the early seventeenth century that tea was cultivated in Java where the Dutch adopted the word and some samples and carried them to Europe and the British Isles.

Nineteenth-century English writer Ernest Bramah wrote that "it is a mark of insincerity of purpose to spend one's time in looking for the sacred Emperor in the low-class tea-shops." If the said emperor be Chinese, I'm afraid that Bramah is wrong in his supposition that a search for the Emperor down-market is futile, for the word "tea" can be traced back to the Chinese dialect of Amoy (what is today southern Fujian) where it was rendered as *te*. This word was then borrowed into Malay as *te* or *teh*, and eventually by Dutch traders as *thé*. It was originally pronounced "tay" as well as "tee," but the latter eventually won out. Tea was first sold publicly in England at Garway's Coffee House in London, where, as we know from his diary entry of September 25, 1660, Samuel Pepys was introduced to the brew: "I did send for a cup of *tee* (a China drink) of which I never had drank before."

In 1661, the drinking of tea was introduced into high society by Queen Catherine, the Portuguese wife of Charles II. Before long, the price fell and the hoi polloi joined in the tea craze — two cups of tea daily became the norm in England.

❧ TOTE

According to David K. Barnhart and Allan A. Metcalf's *America in So Many Words*, within fifty years of the first settlers arriving in America, dialect differences appeared between North and South. Northerners said "carry"; Southerners said "tote." In 1677, the soldiers in Virginia were commanded "to goe to work, fall trees . . . and toat rails, which many of them refusing to doe, he presently disarm'd them." Given the skewed division of labour that existed in seventeenth-century America one can rest assured that much of the heavy toting was awarded to black slaves. In fact, the word "tote" probably derives from *tota* or *tuta*, "to pick up," or "to carry," that is found in the Bantu languages of Africa. The word may have been absorbed into English through the Gullah dialect prevalent in South Carolina and Georgia, which has also provided us with "juke" (as in juke-box) and "mojo." By all accounts, the use of "tote" in today's American South is not particularly prevalent.

The use of the term "tote bag," however, to refer to a large handbag or shoulder bag is common in most English-speaking areas dating back to the beginning of the twentieth century. Also, "gun-toting" is widespread, particularly in headlines.

TYCOON

Who was the first tycoon? The word first arrived in English in the nineteenth century, but if you guess Andrew Carnegie or J.D. Rockefeller you would be wrong. The first tycoon was the shogun of Japan. The first citation of this word in the *OED* in 1857 comes from T. Harris' *Diary*: "I am told *Ziogoon* is not the proper appellation of their ruler, but that it is *Tykoon*. *Ziogoon* is literally 'Generalissimo' while *Tykoon* means 'Great Ruler.'" Ultimately, the word can be traced back to Chinese where *ta* means "great" and *kiun* means "prince." By the early 1860s it actually became a nickname for Abraham Lincoln and shortly thereafter it was used to refer to a dominant or important person. By the end of the nineteenth century it had acquired its modern meaning of a magnate of industry.

VICARIOUS

If you divide this word after the letter "r" you obtain "vicar" and "ious," with the "IOU" being a written acknowledgement of debt. This humorous faux-etymology fits in nicely with the word's origins, as it would appear that "vicarious" was originally used to refer to a debt coming from Christianity, if not directly from the vicar. The first *OED* citation in the seventeenth century states, "If I . . . religiously adore before the Pastor, as the Vicarious Signe of Christ himself." Also, the *OED* points out that frequently in theology, the word is used with reference to the suffering and death of Christ. For example, Reverend Joseph Gilbert's nineteenth-century book *The Christian Atonement* refers to the "Christian doctrine of vicarious expiation."

VILLAIN

Please do not use the words "farmer" or "peasant" in a pejorative sense, because to do so is to partake in an age-old practice of demeaning agricultural workers. Many words that were originally value-neutral and referred merely to country folk have degraded over the centuries. In this category we have all the following: "boor," "pagan," "churl," "yokel" and "villain." Villain, for example, comes from the medieval villa where an uneducated *villein* (from Latin *villanus*), "serf," toiled in his lord's fields as a farm labourer. The term was first used at the end of the eleventh century, and almost immediately its use implied the supposed depraved, unprincipled nature of the worker.

BIBLIOGRAPHY

Ammer, Christine. *Fighting Words*. Chicago: NTC Publishing, 1999.

Ayto, John. *Dictionary of Word Origins*. New York: Arcade Publishing, 1990.

Barber, Katherine. *Six Words You Never Knew Had Something to Do with Pigs*. Don Mills, ON: Oxford University Press, 2006.

Barnhart Concise Dictionary of Etymology. New York: Harper Collins, 1985.

Beeton, Isabella. *Book of Household Management*. Adelaide: S.O. Beeton, 1861.

Blount, Roy. *Alphabet Juice*. New York: Sarah Crichton Books, 2008.

Braudel, Fernand. *A History of Civilization*. Translated by Richard Mayne. London: Penguin, 1995.

Brown-Driver-Briggs-Gesenius Hebrew-English Lexicon. Peabody, MA: Hendrickson Publishers, 1985.

Bryson, Bill. *Made in America*. New York: Morrow, 1994.

Canadian Oxford Dictionary. Don Mills, ON: Oxford University Press, 2004.

Canadian Oxford Paperback Thesaurus. Don Mills, ON: Oxford University Press, 2003.

Chaucer, Geoffrey, *The Canterbury Tales*. Edited by Derek Albert Pearsall. London: G. Allen & Unwin, 1985.

Crystal, David. *The Cambridge Encyclopedia of the English Language*. Cambridge: 1997.

Crystal, David & Ben. *Shakespeare's Words*. London: Penguin, 2002.

Encarta World English Dictionary. 2nd ed. New York: St. Martin's Press, 2004.

Fee, Margery & Janice McAlpine. *Guide to Canadian English Usage*. Don Mills, ON: Oxford University Press, 2007.

Frank, Francis Wattman & Paula A. Treichler. *Language, Gender and Professional Writing*. New York: MLA Publishing, 1988.

Funk, Wilfred. *Word Origins and Their Romantic Stories*. New York: Bell Publishing, 1978.

Grose, Francis. *A Classical Dictionary of the Vulgar Tongue*. Menston, UK: Scolar Press, 1968.

Hendrickson, Robert. *The Facts on File Encyclopedia of Word and Phrase Origins*. New York, 1997.

Hitchens, Henry. *The Secret Life of Words*. New York: FSG, 2008.

Holy Scriptures. Tel-Aviv: Sinai Publishing, 1979.

Hughes, Geoffrey. *Words in Time*. Cambridge: Blackwell, 1988.

Jacobs, Jay. *The Eaten Word*. New York: Birch Lane Press, 1995.

Jones, Sir William. *The Sanscrit Language*. Calcutta, India, 1786.

Lederer, Richard. *The Miracle of Language*. New York: Simon & Schuster, 1991.

Liberman, Anatoly. *Word Origin*. New York: Oxford University Press, 2005.

Longfellow, Henry W. *The Poetic Works of Henry W. Longfellow*. Boston: Houghton Mifflin, 1891.

Oxford English Dictionary Online. Oxford: Oxford University Press, 2000.

Oxford Dictionary of Word Histories. Oxford: Oxford University Press, 2002.

Morris, William. *Morris Dictionary of Word and Phrase Origins*. New York: Harper & Row, 1988.

Quinion, Michael. *Ologies and Isms*. Oxford: Oxford University Press, 2002.

––––––. *Posh and Other Language Myths*. London: Penguin, 2004.

Rawson, Hugh. *Devious Derivations*. New York: Crown Publishers, 1994.

Richler, Howard. *Global Mother Tongue: The Eight Flavours of English*. Montreal: Véhicule Press, 2006.

Room, Adrian. *Room's Classical Dictionary: The Origins of the Names of Characters in Classical Mythology*. London: Routledge & Kegan Paul, 1983.

Rosten, Leo. *The New Joys of Yiddish*. New York: Crown Publishers, 2002.

Shakespeare, William. *The Complete Works of William Shakespeare*. New York: Books Inc, 1956.

Shipley, Joseph. *Dictionary of Word Origins*. New York: NY Philosophical Library, 1945.

Tulloch, Alexander. *Word Routes: Journeys through Etymology*. London: Peter Owen, 2005.

Webster's Dictionary of Word Origins. New York: Smithmark Publishers, 1995.

Webster's Third International Dictionary. Springfield: Merriam-Webster, 1993.

Weekly, Ernest. *An Etymological Dictionary of Modern English*. New York: Dover, 1967.

INDEX

ABOUT THE AUTHOR

Howard Richler is a longtime logophile who has served as a language columnist for several newspapers and magazines. He is the author of five previous books on language: *The Dead Sea Scroll Palindromes* (1995), *Take My Words: A Wordaholic's Guide to the English Language* (1996), *A Bawdy Language: How a Second-Rate Language Slept Its Way to the Top* (1999), *Global Mother Tongue: The Eight Flavours of English* (2006), and most recently *Can I Have a Word with You?* (2007). Richler is now working on three books: one is an analysis of wit in the English language; another explains the magic of word origins and is directed toward children age nine to fifteen; still another is a collection of word puzzles he has created that he guarantees will forestall the onset of dementia. Richler makes his home in Montreal.